THE CINNAMON STICK
Tales of the Spice Trade

PRINTED IN THE UNITED STATES OF AMERICA

Booklocker.com, Inc.
2002

Written by Letta Meinen
Edited by Cynthia Fell and
Margaret Beardmore
Photographs by Letta Meinen
Copyright free Graphics
Pictures provided by
McCormick & Company, Inc.
Recipe provided by
Tones Spice Company

THE CINNAMON STICK
Tales of the Spice Trade

Letta Meinen

Dedicated to my husband and best friend Bill.
He is the wind beneath my wings.

Table of Contents

THE CINNAMON STICK

Tales of the Spice Trade

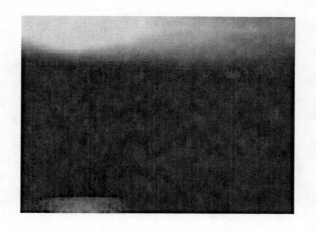

PART 1

IN THE BEGINNING

THE RISE OF A RAGE

We can all remember when new products were introduced we know how expensive they were, but we just had to have them anyway. There is always a rush to purchase these new items, no matter what the price. You soon realize that as more of the products become available the price soon goes down. These high prices are caused by a large demand with a small supply. This desire for being the first to own a new product is called "a rage". A rage is a fad or a passion to the owner of these items. This desire or rage was part of the early Mediterranean civilization when spices became the rage and the pursuit of them lasted for thousands of years.

The first authentic records of the use of spices date from the Mesopotamian and Egyptian kingdoms about 2,600 B. C. In these early ages, these spices reached the Mediterranean area by the practice of trading goods or barter. Merchants took excess products and traveled to distant places to exchange them for wares not found in their area. In these early times, nomad tribes in Arabia dealt in the trade of Frankincense and Myrrh aromatic resins gathered in southern Arabia. The Arabs were frequent traders in the markets along the Mediterranean Sea, Persian Gulf and on the coast of India. In these early days, people did not travel too far, but the nomad traders were known to travel long distances along their trade routes by camel, mules or on foot. When they traded with merchants in India they were introduced to cinnamon and cassia.

In reality, cinnamon and cassia grew in India and the Far East. It was the inner bark of two different evergreen trees. The Arabs traded for these spices at the markets on the west coast of India. Using dhows (Arabian boats), they followed the Indian coastline to the seaports collecting their bundles of spices. The tribes used caravans of camels and donkeys as they traveled from the southern part of Arabia, north through the desert and mountainous regions to the people living along the Mediterranean Sea.

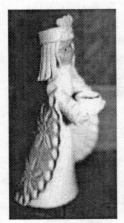

Religious leaders in these early days were known to use ointments and incense for a special sacraments and caring for the dead. Spices were prized as medicines, perfumes, flavorings, and of fumigants. Since they were so scarce, only religious leaders were rich enough to purchase such aromatics. When the Arabs brought the new rare spices to the markets, they were valued so highly that they were traded for gold, silver and jewels. We can understand why these spices were such a treasure, a recipe found in the Bible of sacred oils and incense was used by the holy men of the temples, to anoint and bless holy items.

Exodus 30: 22-24. Moreover, the Lord said to Moses. Take the finest spices: or liquid myrrh 500 shekel, and of the sweet smelling cinnamon half as much, that of 250, and of aromatic cane 250, and of cassia 500, according to the shekel of the sanctuary, and of olive oil a bin" and you shall make of these a sacred anointing oil blended as by a perfumer, a holy anointing oil it shall be.

There is another formula for incense using spices also found in Exodus 30: 34-35. It was used as a burned offering on altars and in religious ceremonies. The burning of incense was believed to cleanse the temples and holy places of evil spirits. It was believed unpleasant odors were associated with evil. While sweet, clean scents were linked with purity and goodness. Thus, a demand was created to ward off evil spirits and to please the Gods.

The practice of embalming in early days grew out of the belief that the deceased would return to their normal duties in the life after. Large quantities of spices were used in preparing the bodies for burial. The procedure was to fill the body cavity with aromatics and spices, then wrap it in spice-soaked strips of cloths. This method would preserve the body in its natural likeness. Professional embalmers and lesser priests were in charge of these burials rituals. Funeral rites also included the burning of incense to appease the Gods of the dead. Nero, Emperor of Rome, burned a years' supply of cinnamon at a ceremony for the death of his wife.

In these early times Religious leader, known as Physicians, supervised the treatment and healing of the people. They gave treatments using prayers and healing herbs and spices. Clay tablets excavated from the ruins of the city of Nippur in Mesopotamia River Valley, revealed medical records on the uses of seeds, roots, resins and bark. It showed how they stored the solid and powdered spices. These clay tablets also described a soothing ointment of powdered spices mixed with wine and oils to relieve aches and pains. Ashes of burned plants and spices were mixed with natural fat and used as an antiseptic soap. When the authority of the church weakened, the development of medicines became more scientific and physicians became known primarily as healers. Hioppocrates, a Greek medical man of 400 B.C., listed plants and spices with directions on how to prepare them for treatment. Physicians became known as the "Father of Medicines".

As the population increased, so did the demand for spices. The Arabian merchants who transported these products became rich. The Royalty was known to use elaborate amounts of spices as the Romans were the most extravagant. It was a morning ritual to go to the scented baths to relax. While in the baths, they would sip spiced wines along with food and entertainment. They were given spiced oil massages to keep their skin supple. Spiced perfumes and cosmetics were desired by the ladies to make themselves more attractive. Many oiled their hair and bound flowers and spices into it to keep it sweet smelling for a long time. The baths were the center of Roman social life.

The Arabian tribesmen spent many days traveling from market to market in the desert country. In contrast to the Romans elaborate baths, the Arabs used a makeshift sauna to cleanse themselves. Using a clay pot or a hole dug in the ground, they placed spices and aromatic resins on hot coals. They crouched over this smoldering substance with their robes spread like a tent to keep the fumes inside. This produced heavy sweating which cleansed the skin and fumigated their robes.

We understand the people's desire to acquire spices to offset the unpleasant aromas of the time. It is no wonder they believed that unpleasant odors were evil and sweet smelling spices were a purifier.

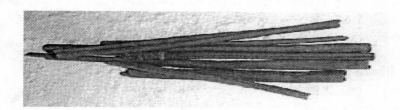

THE ARABS – MASTER SPICE TRADER

From earliest times until today the Arab's are an interesting subject. The Arabs were a resourceful group. They lived in tribes with the eldest man the head of each household. He was known as the Sheik and he controlled his family and their business. The Arabian Peninsula was covered with these tribes and they were usually nomads roaming around the country for food and water for their people and their flock. It was only fitting that they became merchants, as they successfully domesticating the donkeys and camels to carry their goods. The camel could travel great distances without water and could carry 500 pounds of merchandise.

It was common in the Third Century B. C. for the Arabs to be known as eloquent speakers and great story tellers. By these stories it was their way of preserving their history to the young of their tribes. The Sheiks believed in the Arabic Proverb that the worth of a man lies in the eloquence of his tongue. The market always drew a cross section of people from the Mediterranean countries. In this way, news of far places and trade was carried to all section of the area. It was common for the merchants, after a hectic day of trading to gather in groups to tell stories. The Sheik could hold his listeners spellbound by his stories of their adventures and travels.

The Sheik was a colorful character, with his long flowing robes and headdress. His eyes flashed with tales of the adventures of caravans encountering dangers of many kinds in acquiring his wares. He could wave large bundles of cinnamon in the faces of the gathered group, extolling on its sweetness and priceless commodity. He could elaborate on the dangers his workers encountered in harvesting these fragile sticks. He told of wild animals, ferocious large winged birds that would attack the workers making these spices so valuable. The Sheiks make the Priests believe that these spices were sacred and untouched by human hands. They were told that the priests should sacrifice the first bundle of cinnamon or cassia to appease the gods.

For thousands of years, the merchants of the Mediterranean Kingdoms believed these bizarre stories. These tales were made up by the Arabs to keep their spice supply secret. They wanted a monopoly on its trade so the riches they acquired in exchange of good would be theirs alone. The spice supply was the best kept secret in history as the noted Greek Scholar Herodotus writing about strange lands and customs described cassia as, grown in shallow swamps, protected by winged animals, like huge bats. By these outlandish lies, the Arabs were able to protect their source of supply of cinnamon and cassia.

To understand the Arab people, we must believe the anthropologist who states that these people are descendants of the

Semitic tribes who roamed the Arabian Desert. The Arab people are known to be intense and volatile and lived on a moral code emphasizing courage and tribal loyalty. The law of the desert was "an eye for an eye, a tooth for a tooth." They held grudges for years if they felt an insult was made to their pride, and bloody feuds followed. They had no courts and jails but misconduct by any member was dealt with harshly.

Many Arabs tribes migrated to Egypt, Mesopotamia, Syria, Jordon and Canaan. Throughout the centuries their influence spread as they mingled with the established kingdoms or started new nations. Arab scribes and moneychangers in these countries became prominent in their respected nations. In the Mesopotamia markets, the Arabs developed a cuneiform writing on clay tablets to help in recording trade transactions. The remaining tribes

stayed in the desert and Yemen in southern Arabia and became the wealthy sea and caravan traders.

The dress of the nomadic men and woman changed little throughout time. They wore a knee-high shirt with a sash over which they wore an ankle length robe. They tied a shawl over their head to protect their face from the desert sun, sand and wind. The men were considered superior and they made all the decisions of their business and the caravans. The women had secondary roles and cared for the smaller animals. They managed the household and cared for the children. Their duties entailed using a loom to weave cloth, a mortar and pestle to grind grain, and clay pots for cooking. The families lived in tents and were a hearty resourceful people being able to move about the desert with ease. They were called Bedouin (known as desert dweller) with these caravans, and the Arabs became a familiar sight on the desert roads of Arabia, which became known as the Spice and Incense Routes.

CARAVANS AND THE SPICE ROUTE

Consider that your family is planning a trip of 1600 miles from Omaha, Nebraska to Disneyland in California. You will be driving 3-4 days over Interstate Highways, staying in comfortable motels with many choices of food. Compare this to a trip taken in the first century on the Spice Route by the Arabian family. They would be part of a caravan that is a long train of slow moving camels and humanity traveling the same 1,600 miles from Southern Arabia to the Mediterranean Sea. This same trip for the Arab family could take 40-70 days.

The Spice Route of Arabia traveled by the caravans was one of the oldest in history. It is located 100 miles inland from the Red Sea and meanders from Yemen in Southern Arabia north to Petra in Jordon. At Petra, the caravan divides with one group going into Egypt and the other moving east to Syria. This spice route crosses a vast area of barren country, plains, mountains and desert. Along the route oasis with spring water was found making a welcome place for the caravans to stop. The caravans passed often through these barren areas, which allowed robbers or hostile tribes demanding toll from them before they could pass through. In other places, friendly tribes welcomed them with festivals and warm greetings with much trading of goods.

Each caravan had one master, usually the Sheik of a prominent tribe. Preparation for this annual trip north took the Sheik from three to four months to organize. He would need to contact merchants who wished to carry their goods to the Mediterranean markets. He needed to hire overseers, guards, couriers, camel drivers and servants. He collected funds to cover all tariffs and tolls that would need to be paid along the route.

The caravans were divided into companies, with an overseer in charge of each unit. There would be several companies to each caravan because banding together in large groups meant safety in numbers. They usually assembled in a common place where they camped for a week or more to prepare for the long journey. A large caravan could include 6,000 people with animals outnumbering the people. Most were camels, but goats, donkeys and sheep were needed for food and trade. When this mass of humanity and animals gathered, confusion was the order of the day with bellowing camels, shouting overseers, sweating and cursing laborers and people scurrying in all directions. When the day to leave arrives, order was established and the caravan stretches out two miles long.

The camels were known as "ships of the desert" and carried all the merchandise for trade plus all the belongings of the Arab families. It is known that the Arabs would ship 3,000 tons of merchandise annually for the markets at the Mediterranean. Prominent families of the southern area make the trip north and will provide their own camels. These camels would be fitted with a litter to carry their family and supplies. The litters were built to fit atop the camel and were decorated with colorful cloth and brass ornaments. The Sheik in charge of the caravan would be in front

of the caravan where he was fitted with a special litter with two camels one behind the other. His camels would be fitted with bells and the sound of the bells made the servants sing as they walked along. The poorer class of people rode on rugs spread on top of boxes
and bales of merchandise on the camels. The remainder of the workers and servants walked beside their charges, it all must have made an amazing sight.

The Couriers of the caravan were communicators as they rode ahead to alert villagers and tribes of the approaching caravan. Some villagers quickly organized a fair or festival to make ready items to trade, as the caravan would need fruits, vegetables, meat and gifts. The villagers beat drums to signal the approaching caravan and to welcome the travelers. If the couriers found hostile tribes the caravan was alerted and tolls were paid for safe passage, then a rider from this tribe would lead the caravan through safely. Wars between tribes were frequent and the caravan tried to wait out the danger whenever they could. Pliny, the Roman Scholar, is known to have written, that caravans packed with merchandise were forbidden to turn aside from the main route. Travelers had to stick to this Spice and Incense Route for their own safety.

The veil of secrecy concerning the Spice trade was finally lifted when an Indian sailor stranded in the Red Sea offered to show Eudozus, a Greek seaman the route to India. They made a successful trip to the west coast of India and upon his return; Eudozus gave a description of trade and travel in the Arabian Sea. He told of the exports of masses amounts of cinnamon and cassia sold to the Arabian seaman in the Indian ports. With the Spice secret finally uncovered, it opened new trade to adventurous sailors. On these trips they encountered ferocious storms, shipwrecks and pirates. Even with all these dangers, numerous ships made the trip to India and on to the Far East to reap the many riches spices brought in trade.

IN KEEPING WITH THE TIMES WITH CINNAMON

YOGURT

This creamy concoction was discovered thousands of years ago. Legend has it that a nomad who tucked some milk in his goatskin bag and slung it across his camel. When he opened the

13

bag hours later he found this tasty, tangy custard. The hot weather along with the culture of the goatskin soon made his milk a staple along the traveled routes of the nomad tribes.

Yogurt can be made from any type of milk by adding a small amount of cultured yogurt to heated milk you can make your own yogurt at home. Depending on the amount you want to try, use clean covered jars and pour the same measured amount of milk in a pan and bring to near boiling. When using a Yogurt maker it comes with a temperature guide so no guesswork is needed. This guide shows the right temperature to cool the milk and the time to add a small amount of previously made yogurt or from commercial yogurt with active cultures. Place in jars and cover, keep in a warm area with no drafts and within hours you will have a tasty yogurt. If using a Yogurt maker it gives suggested time to properly incubate your yogurt.

RECIPES USING YOGURT

SWEET CINNAMON YOGURT

1-cup container of Yogurt
1-teaspoon of sugar
½-teaspoon of cinnamon
1-teaspoon of wheat germ

Place Yogurt in small bowl and add remaining ingredients and mix well. Place in refrigerator to cool and firm up. Serve in dessert dish topped with sliced strawberries and a dash of cinnamon.

YOGURT CREAM CHEESE

1-cup container of yogurt

Place in cheesecloth layers or into a large coffee pot liner and tie the top together and hold with a rubber band. Place yogurt in strainer and lay the strainer over a medium size container. Place in the refrigerator to drain for 3-4 days. Test to see if Yogurt is firm to the touch, when it feels solid it is ready to use.

A suggestion on how you can spice up this cream cheese, before you place in the cheesecloth bag, add cinnamon, peanut butter and finely chopped nuts to your taste and mix well. Continue with same instruction as above. Both of these spreads are great on your morning toast, bagel or muffins.

RECIPE FOR A ROAST "IN" THE FIRE

On their many travels the nomads cooked their meats in holes dug in the ground and placed their meat amongst the coals to cook. We haven't come too far, except we use a grill and charcoal briquettes. I used this method of cooking meat for friends and family some years ago and it always amazed our guests. I made this for a dinner when our oldest daughter was married in 1970. She prepared a 10 pound rolled beef roast for her guest when her son got married in July of 2002. She has made this often for her friends and as she says, there was never a scrap left over. I made this smaller version just so I could get the pictures to show the progression of preparing a roast in a clay mold tossed in the fire.

2-pound beef roast round or oval shaped
4-cups flour
½-cup of yellow mustard
1-cup rock salt
1-can beer any brand

 The amount of this mixture may vary according to the size of the roast you will be covering. We live in a Condo and my grill is rather small so this is the size I used. Blend all above ingredients in a large bowl and stir to make a consistency of modeling clay adding more or less of the beer. Use only enough beer so the clay is not too dry or too moist.

On a clean surface place completely chilled beef roast, dry meat completely with paper towels. Take part of your clay mixture and pat firmly around all sides. Pinch seems together so no part of roast is visible. Place in refrigerator to firm up clay mold.

Once you have completed the above mixture, prepare your grill with 2-3 pounds of charcoal briquettes. Place in cone shape in middle of grill and light. While charcoal is reaching that white-hot stage, prepare your tools for working with clay mold. Use long  tongs, heavy oven mitts, hammer, long fork and receptacle for mold.

When coals are white-hot using tongs arrange coals to cover bottom of grill. Remove clay mold from refrigerator and toss into coals in one corner of grill. Leave for 20-25 minutes, then with long tongs roll clay roast one-fourth turn to another spot on the charcoal. Remove any coals that may be stuck to clay. In another 20-25 minutes move roast again to another spot. After the final 20-25 minutes, which will be the fourth turn, remove your blackened clay roast to a sturdy table with receptacle to hold the hot clay mold. Be sure to use insulated oven mitts to handle clay. Take a hammer and break open clay mold, remove roast with long fork and place on platter. Experiment with this different way to cook a roast.

NEEDLE WEAVING

The Arab women were known to use looms to weave their cloth for their garments and head coverings. The loom the Arab women used was a device of two long poles that held their warp cords. The one pole was tied close to their body while the other pole was attached to a solid object such as a tent stake. They would start their weaving at this lower pole near their body continuing as far as they could reach. Then they would roll the pole over the finished work and continue weaving. When it was time to depart on the caravan they would roll the loom and have it ready to work on at the next stop. Imagine this loom similar to a hammock. This type of loom was easy to use while they traveled the caravan route. They used wool spun in course yarns from the animals that accompanied their caravans. Today one can learn the art of weaving by using a cardboard loom with cords and a variety of yarns. Cinnamon sticks make an interesting touch to your finished weaving and gives a pleasant scent.

Weaving is interlocking horizontal yarns called weft, between stationary vertical cords called warp. A loom is a device that holds the warp cords taunt as the warp cords are threaded unto the loom. The warp cords must not stretch, so use a thin strong cotton, linen or nylon cord. The filler or weft yarns can be any type of knitting yarns or even torn narrow stripes of colorful cloth. I have added cinnamon stick into weaving and used a long cinnamon stick at the top to finish off the weaving.

Following is a list of material and directions for a cardboards loom and wall hanging.

Find heavy corrugated cardboard (6" by 14"), pencil, ruler, scissor and transparent tape. Thin strong cord and string for warp cord, knitting yarns for weft cord in your favorite colors that will accent the cinnamon stick. Needles used can be in a variety of shapes, but ones with a large eye with a blunt end are recommended. I have used large plastic ones plus wooden or metal flat ones with large eyes to hold a mixture of yarns.

Loom Directions – using materials given in above directions. Draw a line across each 6" side of cardboard down ½" from the top and bottom of loom. Place pencil marks ¼" apart across both top and bottom of the 6-inch side of the loom. You will have 22 marks on each top and bottom. Cut marks to the ½" line with a scissor.

To warp your loom use thin strong string or cord, place end of cord in first notch, make a knot in end and tape to back of loom. Pull cord taunt without bending your cardboard down to the bottom of loom and hook around first and second notches. Continue to top of loom and hook around second and third notches. Continue in this manner until all notches are filled using even tension throughout. Knot last cord and tape to back of loom.

 Follow the direction for making fringe for bottom of wall hanging. Cut 48 strands of yarn 18" long, can be a mixture of colors you have picked for your weaving. Starting at the bottom of loom you will place Rya knots across the width of the loom. The Rya stitch is a knot wound around two warp cords. The long tails of this stitch will create the fringe.

Using four strands of yarn for each Rya stitch take one end of the four stands and slip around first warp cord. Slip the other end around the second cord and take both ends and gently pull these strands to bottom of loom to tighten know. Repeat this stitch across first row you will have eleven groups of knots. Work second row or Rya stitches with remaining strands. You will have 10 groups of knots on this row. Trim uneven strands of fringe with scissor.

The following directions are for weaving the body of wall hanging. Cut four strands of one color yarn 72" long, do not stretch yarn when measuring. Thread yarn on the blunt needle and begin weaving a tabby stitch. This stitch is interlacing the yarn over and under the warp cords across the loom. Gently pull yarn through, leaving a small end to anchor around the first warp cord. 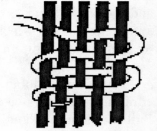 Continue second row with this tabby stitch, alternating the over and under to interlock the previous row. Remember do not pull weft yarns tight leave enough tension so sides of weaving do not pull in. Complete this pattern using all the yarn ending with a full row. Secure end around warp cord. Using fingers push down the rows of yarn to bottom of loom, so no warp cords show through.

The next step in working your weaving is using an accent color of yarn. Cut 16 strands of this yarn 10" long. Thread four strands on needle and weave tabby stitch across warp cords. Center the strands and let ends hang along the sides of weaving. Repeat this tabby stitch for a second row. Use a cinnamon stick and alternate the over and under across loom. Using the remaining yarns repeat two more rows above and let the ends hang along side of weaving. Continue the above directions until you reach the top of the loom.

Follow directions carefully for removing weaving from your loom. Push down finished weaving until you have over 4" of warp cords remaining at the top. This is so you can tie off the warp ends and have enough to tie in your last cinnamon stick. This stick will create a firm top so you can hang your weaving as a wall hanging. To remove your weaving from the loom cut the first two war p cords. With the warp cords you taped down, tie it to one of the ones you cut and tie firmly to top of weaving. Continue cutting and tying as you go across your loom until all cords are tied. Place your cinnamon stick along the top and place one warp cord in front of the stick and one behind, knot these two together in back of weaving. Continue across loom until all are tied in back. Trim excess yarn from back of weaving. To remove the bottom of your weaving from the loom, fold your weaving away from the loom and gently remove the warp cords from the bottom of the loom. You now have completed your first weaving. You can make a small look of yarn in the center of the cinnamon stick to hang on the wall. Check the following instruction on how to make a twisted rope from yarn for a hanger including other suggestions.

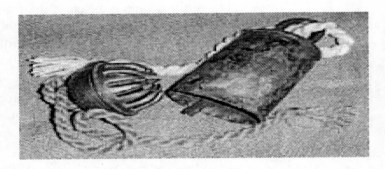

TWISTED ROPE

Twisted rope can be made in all sizes depending on the amount of yarn you begin with. Large twisted ropes make decorative belts. Possible that is how the Arabs used to tie up their tunics or a band to hold their head dress in place. Make rope and tassels to hang you're weaving following the instruction below.

Cut 4 strands of worsted 4 ply yarn in 6-yard lengths. Do not stretch yarn while measuring. Fold in half and place folded part over a hook and begin twisting yarn starting close to the hook and twisting in one direction. Continue pulling the yarn as you twist and continue twisting tightly until the end leaving 2 inches for fringe. Walk to where you started at the hook holding twisted yarn at arms length. Place these ends together as you remove yarn from your hook and let your yarns become twisted onto each other. Tie the loose ends together, using a 6-inch piece of yarn and wrapping it around the rope 3-inches from the end. Clip the folded end of the rope and repeat the directions given above for tying off the rope. Trim the fringe tassel areas on both ends and you will have a 22-inch length of rope. Tie this rope on each end of the cinnamon stick and your weaving is ready to hang. If you prefer extra tassels follow directions below for making tassels.

If you want to make a belt but extra thickness of yarn and make it four times the length you want the finished product. If you want an easy belt place the tied end around your waist and slip the knotted end through the loop at the other end. Pull tight or keep loose around the hips. By combining colors and kinds of yarn you can make many colorful accessories such as lanyards for necklaces using this method.

TASSELS

Cut a cardboard the length you want your tassels. Wind yarn around this length numerous times for a thick tassel. Using a 12-inch piece of yarn slip under yarn on cardboard and tie all yarns together firmly at the tip. Using a scissor clip the bottom yarns from the cardboard. Hold all tassels yarns together and wrap a 6-inch piece of yarn an inch from the top, wind firmly and tie off. Trim bottom yarns to even the yarns of the tassel. These tassels can be made in different sizes and used in many types of decorations. The Arabs must have used this method to decorate their garments and also their camels. They loved to decorate the camels with fringes, tassels and bells. Many camels were elaborately decorated when they were on the Caravans.

As much as our world changes and grows…much of it stays the same.   Letta ☺

THE CINNAMON STICK

Tales of the Spice Trade

PART 2

WATERWAYS AND WARFARE

SPICES AND THE WATERWAYS

A mass of humanity jammed the harbor of Muziris on the Malabar Coast of India. Ships crashed and bumped into each other. Shell horns honked constantly as ships tried to find a docking place to moor. The sea in 100 A.D. had become a wide opening into the world. Great cities sprang up wherever trading became popular. The world was expanding and sailing was the fastest known way to travel.

The noisy shouts of sailors and merchants were heard from morning till night along with constant pounding of shipbuilders trying to keep up with the demand for new ships. The rowdy crowds pushed and shoved as they moved along the pier. Amidst this chaos, the blending of peoples was astounding. Dark skinned Africans, gray-bearded Sheiks of Arabia, fair-skinned Mediterranean, turban-bound Indians, plus a mixture of merchants, sailors, slaves and servants from all parts of the known world. Such was the scene at the busy harbor of Muziris. It had become the gateway to the world. As fast as one ship sailed out, other ships sailed in. It was recorded as the port where large ships from the north brought gold and silver to trade for the valuable spices of India.

The main interest of the throngs of people was the market place. It was situated close to the harbor, along narrow, crooked streets. Shops were in recessed areas of buildings with booths set up under awnings in the spaces along the streets. Perfumers, skilled in the use of aromatics and spices, were a welcome relief from the stench of the markets. Bales of cinnamon and cassia drew many interested Roman buyers. Burlap bags of spices disappeared as merchants from Greece and Arabia carried off this valuable product. Roman and Greek coins were standard currency during this time. Traders carried scales or balancers to weigh the coins for proper exchange of goods.

The western traders were familiar figure in the Indian ports. Many Arab and Jewish merchants stayed in Muziris to set up trade centers. Their influence helped develop the Malabar Coast to become an industrious area that thrived as an international meeting a
place. The waterways that brought these people to the Malabar Coast were known as the "Spice Route" of the oceans. This route was not a single lane, but resembled a spider web. The water routes fed in all directions, with India at the center. The northern and western routes went to the Persian Gulf, Red Sea and the east coast of Africa. They crisscrossed the Arabian Sea and Indian Ocean. The southern and eastern routes went to Ceylon (now Sri Lanka), The Indonesian Islands, Malaysia and China. They crisscrossed the Bay of Bengal and the China Sea.

The first Mediterranean seaman to discover the monsoon winds was the Greek merchant, Hippalus, in 40 A.D. This led the Greeks and Romans to begin to build ships on a larger scale. The demand for spices continued to be so strong that the Europeans wanted to trade directly with the Indian merchants. The great ships from the Rome and Greece could make the trip from the Red Sea to the Malabar Coast in 40 days, using the monsoon winds. These big ships brought gold from the African coast and returned to Rome laden with cinnamon, cassia and pepper, silks and pearls from India.

The monsoon winds were an early discovery of the Indian and Arabian seamen. It helped them to produce extensive sea trade by using these winds to cross the Arabian Sea. These winds blew cool, dry air from the north and east in winter. With the ships leaving the Arabian ports in November, they were able to sail directly to the Malabar Coast. In December, after the cyclone season had passed, they sailed around Ceylon and crossed the Bay of Bengal to Malaysia. The ships would continue trading in Indonesian ports until the winds reversed in April and warm humid air came from the south and west continuing into the summer. The ships then sailed with these southern winds up the China Sea and to the port of Canton, China. Here, the ships had to wait until the north monsoon winds came before starting their return voyage. These trips usually took two years to complete. All these natural trade winds helped the early sailors sail on the Spice Route waterways to build their fortune, in cinnamon, cassia, pepper and the riches of the Far East.

The Indian sailors were the first to sail through the hazard of open water by sailing in both directions on the Spice Route

waterways. These early seamen sailed by using birds. They let the birds loose at intervals and would follow the course they took to land. The Arab seamen, on the other hand, became knowledgeable astronomers and navigated by using the stars on long ocean voyages.

Sea travel was not without danger as the Red Sea and the Persian Gulf posed many problems. There were few harbors, treacherous breakers and rocks, plus strong winds. Shipwrecks were common and pirates preyed on trading vessels. Ocean travel held unknown danger with stories of sea monsters and ferocious storms frightened many sailors. In spite of the hazards of traveling by sea, many countries continued to make the dangerous trips to trade for spices.

When the Europeans increased trade with India in 300 A. D., the Arab control of spices gradually declined. The Arabs soon dropped out of shipping in India, and turned to piracy by preying on the European ships. The Arabs continued the overland caravans with a small supply of spices along with the incense they controlled. At this time, the Roman Empire was expanding. After conquering Greece, the Romans utilized the Greek mastery of shipbuilding and sea travel. They used the skilled Greek sailors to expand their trade. This helped the Romans to obtain supremacy of the seas. With the increase in shipbuilding, they took control of the western section of the Spice Route waterways. This enabled the Romans to ship spices back to Rome in record time as spices were still in great demand.

The Romans were obsessive in the use of cinnamon and cassia. They pillaged and conquered nations, forcing them to pay tribute in gold, which was shipped to India in exchange for the desired spices. The spices were so expensive that only the wealthy could afford them. The Romans used them lavishly in every conceivable way. The wealthy Romans and Clergy were sharply criticized by Pliny, the Greek Scholar, for the waste of Rome's gold and silver metals  on useless luxuries such as perfumes, cinnamon, cassia, and silks. He complained that it was draining the Roman Empire of its wealth. This warning proved to be true, as many of the gold and silvers coins from Rome were found on the Malabar Coast in recent times.

Pliny prediction came to pass as the Roman Empire fell into a decline. Western Europe entered into an age of destruction known as the "Dark Ages". This period in European history lasted for many years. With the population increasing, conditions worsened, cities became unbearable with disease and chaos ravaging the lands.

CINNAMON GREED LEADS TO WARFARE

The five hundred years from 400 A.D. to 900 A.D. was one of the worse tragic periods in Western European History. Rome's glory days were fading, as greed and the desire for luxury drained the wealth of the Empire. All parts of the vast Roman Empire were ravaged by wars. Barbaric tribes attacked and burned all civilized areas, including Rome in 476 A.D. What was once thriving cities became divided encampments of people, protecting themselves with fortresses and castles? This period of time in Europe is called the "Dark Ages". For centuries, Europe was a place of stagnation, decaying towns, isolated manors, scattered monasteries and brawling robbers.

The only bright spot in civilization was the Christian Greek-Roman Empire known as the Byzantine Empire. The capital of this Empire was the magnificent city of Constantinople, called "Rome of the East". This city became the center of the spice trade and a crossroads between Asia and Europe. An overland route from China, called the "Silk Road", became a prominent route for trade with Constantinople.

With the unsettled conditions in Europe, only a small amount of spices reached inland. Jewish merchants emerged as pioneers in European trade. They were highly literate and fluent in many languages. They became a link between the tribes and advanced countries, by trading with the castles, monasteries and villages of Europe. The Jews bargained with jewels, cinnamon, cassia and pepper for wool cloth, furs and swords.

In 541 A. D. a devastating plague descended upon the Mediterranean area. This disease originated in Central Africa then moved to Egypt and the surrounding countries. Death traveled swiftly around the Mediterranean countries. Busy ports such as Venice and Constantinople endured dozens of outbreaks. It swirled around the Mediterranean for 200 years, killing 40 million people. In Constantinople the plague killed so many people that the citizens believed it was the end of the world.

The devastation was so appalling that villages were abandoned, agriculture declined, population plunged and trade faltered. Dangers were wide spread; Jews were killed because people thought they poisoned the water. The sick were isolated in houses and later quarantined on islands. There was no escape and no cure and the "Black Plague" was considered the worse natural disaster Europe had ever known. The plague may have been the origin of a gruesome verse that children still recite today:

> Ring around the rosies.
> A pocket full of posies.
> Achoo! Achoo!
> We all fall down.

Rosies were the pink rash associated with the plague, posies were spice nosegays carried and held to their nose to ward off the

 polluted air. The disease brought on sneezing and feverish chills then all would die. With the poor living conditions, the plague flourishes and the infection spread quickly in the crowded filthy cities and homes

Spices became a product of need when the small amount that reached Western Europe was used for the protection of one's health. People of that time believed that the polluted air and fumes were the cause of the disease and they used the spice fumigants to purify the air. Burning pans of spices and aromatics were carried from room to room in hopes of cleansing the air. Sad to say, fresh air was considered dangerous and good sanitation was unknown. . It was common for flea-infested rats to infiltrate the homes. Because hygiene was not practiced, the fleas thrived and were passed along when the clothes of the dead were sold.

At this time, the people did not know the plague was a disease of fleas, carried by rats. After this discovery and the plague began to wane, spices still remained scarce and expensive. People had to lock these valuable spices in chests and cupboards to keep them from being stolen. They appointed trustworthy servants to oversee the distribution and use of the spices. Even with the devastation of the plague in the Mediterranean, trading continued. The Arabs had resumed sea trade with India and the Far East after the fall of Rome in 476 A.D. With the import of the new spices from the Indonesian Islands, the Arabian fortunes increased. The caravan merchants once again carried spices to the Mediterranean seaports.

The Greeks were the first to use a mixture of dried flowers, spices and herbs in which we now call "potpourri". Certain plants have aromas similar to those of expensive and valuable spices. In this way, spices could be extended and stretched. The mixture was thought to have anesthetic qualities and could ward off contamination. People held the nosegays of potpourri to their noses if they came upon obnoxious odors. They also became concerned about tainted foods and turned to spices and pepper to help as a preservative for foods. The Greek herbalists recommended cinnamon for indigestion and a good use as a mouthwash.

The year 600 A.D. was an era of change for the Arabs. Mohammed, a wealthy educated caravan spice merchant from Mecca had the opportunity to visit with many educated men in his travels. He listened and discussed religious beliefs with prominent Jews and Christians. Through much religious meditation, Mohammed felt called to be a messenger of God to his countryman. He founded the new religion, Islam, and became convinced that it was his duty to reveal this religion to his people. Mohammed stressed military force with the belief that all those who would die in battle for his religion would go to heaven and all their wishes would be granted. This religion spread throughout all the areas of the spice trade routes, from the Mediterranean to the Far East.

After Mohammed's death in 632 A. D., the Islamic armies swept through the former Roman Empires, capturing Syria, Egypt, Palestine, North Africa and Spain. This Empire spread from one end of the spice route to the other and along this route many natives were converted to Islam. With the Arab influence and power in trade, the Roman gold and silver coins were soon replaced with Arabian money. A revolutionary change took place in Arabian life. From breeders of camels and being caravan traders, they became princes, generals, governors, judges and rulers of men. They studied astrology, sciences and medicines and were considered the most cultured people of that time.

The march of Islam engulfed a large portion of the Byzantine Empire, especially the Christian religious shrines in Jerusalem. More and more of the Europeans kingdoms became converted to Christianity and people began to take pilgrimages to Jerusalem. With the Arabs in control of vast areas surrounding Jerusalem, great resentment was felt among the European Christian nations. This resentment for Islam and its control of Jerusalem led Europe into crusades warfare starting in 1100 A.D. with the Arabs. The benefit that survived these crusades was surprising to the European nations.

WITNESS OF WEALTH IN WARFARE

From the years 1000 to 1300 there were two important happenings that caused the spice rage to shift to Europe, the crusades and the discovery of wealthy Arabian Countries. Wars were a common occurrence during this time, but massive crusades organized by the European nations against the Arabs were rare. When these crusaders saw the wealth displayed by the Arab countries, it was a surprising experience for the European soldiers.

The desires of people throughout time had not changed. If someone wanted something, they fought for it. The strong overran the weak. After one victory, they wanted ten more, after ten; they wanted a hundred and then the world. No one group was able to conquer the world, because it was bigger than anyone could have imagined. There were always others more powerful and the cycle repeated itself. The usual cause of the strife was the control of trade and the wealth it brought.

With the capture of Jerusalem by the Arabs, European Christians sought to regain their shrine, the tomb of Jesus Christ called the "Holy Sepulchre". Pope Urban II of Rome launched a holy war to recover Jerusalem from Islamic rule. The Pope organized a movement of military pilgrimages called "The Crusades". In 1096, a band of pilgrims began the first Crusade to the Holy Lands but met with disaster. Later the same year, tens of thousands of knights, foot soldiers and pilgrims from around Europe began a march to Jerusalem. In July of 1099 they captured Jerusalem after much bloodshed.

The Crusade allowed the Europeans pilgrims to observe the wealth of the mid-eastern countries. They discovered that the Arabs acquired this wealth from the trading of cinnamon, cassia and other luxury goods. The Crusaders were successful in establishing a Christian colony in Palestine, which helped the Europeans to open trade with Genoa and Venice in Italy that lasted 100 years.

Warfare continued around the Mediterranean when the Turks captured Jerusalem in 1183 and took control of the area. With each threat to the Christian colony, more Crusades of armies from Europe tried to take this colony and Jerusalem but to no avail. The ruling Turks allowed the Christians to remain, which kept the door open for them to continue their trade with Genoa and Venice. A Venetian merchant Geoffrayde Villehardouin participated in the fourth and final Crusade in 1203. Writing about his experiences, he described the riches of the Arab cities and its harbors filled with spices of cinnamon, cassia, furs, precious stones, gold and silver, perfumed wood, carved ivory and jewelry. He was amazed and could not believe there were such riches in the world.

The pilgrims, soldiers and knights that returned to Europe reported with wonder about the living conditions of the mid-eastern countries. They were impressed with the houses, cleanliness, food, knowledge and government. Even with all the destruction of the wars and Crusades,  civilization advanced because of the exchange of ideas. Witnessing the Arab riches started a time of awakening in Europe called the Renaissance, meaning new life or rebirth. To this day the only trace of the Europeans being in this area is the large Christian population still living in Palestine, now called Lebanon.

Venice became part of the trading along one of the old trading routes called the "Silk Road". This road traveled through 17 countries and trading centers along the way became the cross section of caravans exchanging goods. The Europeans became more interested in trading in 1260 when two brothers, Nicolo and Maffio Polo, left Venice for a commercial trip to Bukhara, Uzbekistan, a trading center on the Silk Road. While there, they visited with an envoy sponsored by Kublai Khan, the Emperor of China. This envoy convinced the Polo's to continue the trip on to China. Upon arriving in China, they met the Emperor, the Great

Khan and he was so impressed to meet Europeans, he voiced his desire to trade with Venice and sent a message to the Pope.

In 1271, the Polo Brothers again left Venice for another trip to China taking Nicolo's fifteen-year-old son, Marco. They arrived in China in 1275 and Marco became a favorite of the Emperor. Marco could speak four languages and was sent on official tours throughout the Chinese kingdom. After eleven years of service to Kublai Kahn, the Polo family wanted to return to Venice. On their return voyage by sea, the Kahn outfitted them in splendor with valuable jewels, silks and spices. They arrived in Venice in 1295 and were able to tell about grand civilizations and the abundance of cinnamon and cassia they saw on the many islands they visited. Their families were unbelieving until the travelers displayed all the riches from the Kahn that had been sewn into their clothing to deter frequent encounters of robbers.

In 1298, while visiting in Genoa, Marco Polo was imprisoned during a battle over a trade dispute. While in prison, he told of his experiences in the Far East to another prisoner, Rustchello of Pisa

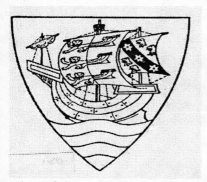

who was a writer of romantic stories. These stories became a book that described the riches of the many lands in which he traveled. Marco described cinnamon, cassia, along with white and black pepper, in great quantities. Marco Polo's book was called "Description of the World". It stunned the Europeans with the tales of the vast amounts of spices. He told of shiploads of pepper in the South China ports with 10,000 pounds coming in daily. He described large spice plantations growing on islands in the China Sea.

It was difficult for the European merchants to believe Marco Polo, because they could not fathom such riches. News such as this was slow to reach the masses, because printing had not yet been invented. Marco Polo's book was copied in long hand and became the most widely read book of its time. It helped arouse the Genoa and Venice merchants to expand their trade with China. Commerce continued to be the driving force of the European economy with Venice and Genoa holding the monopoly on the trade of spices until the late 1300's.

In 1397, Constantinople was captured by the Siljuk Turks, which closed the entry to the Silk Road. Also this overland road was blocked by Mongol tribes, limiting access to the many trade centers along the way to China. The Turkish rulers were not on friendly terms with the Europeans and trade dropped dramatically. Discoveries made by courageous European seamen as they explored new waterways to the Far East causing another challenge to the spice trade.

ACTIVITIES OF THE TIME
CLAY POT CINNAMON BREAD

This recipe will help you get the feel of baking bread in a clay pot like the women of an earlier time. It may be a little work at first preparing your clay pot but you will understand how the early women had to work to prepare their meals on caravans or the servants who handles this detail. Purchase new 6-8 inch tall terra cotta pots, for the cinnamon bread or the low terra cotta pots for cinnamon rolls. Be creative you will find all kinds of terra cotta pots for planting flowers in your favorite garden shop.

SEASONING YOUR TERRA COTTA POT

Wash and rinse clean new terra cotta pots
in the size you wish to work with.
1. Place in warm oven 200 degrees to dry for about 15-20 minutes.
2. Let cool – press foil in bottom of pots to cover bottom hole, smooth evenly for firm fit.
3. With Pastry brush, spread oil inside of pots. Continue spreading oil until no more is absorbed.

41

4. Place pots in 350-degree oven for 15-20 minutes to season pots for baking.
5. Let cool-with pastry brush, coat well inside of pot with margarine.
6. Sprinkle inside with cinnamon-sugar mixture, coating the inside and bottom of pot.
7. Pots are ready for dough

CLAY POT CINNAMON BREAD

2-cups white flour
1-cup whole-wheat flour
1-teaspoon salt
1-package dry yeast
2-tablespoon wheat germ
1-teaspoon cinnamon
¼-teaspoon nutmeg
1 ¼-cup milk
3-tablespoon honey
2-tablespoon oil
½-cup dates or raisins. Chop in small pieces-softened in warm water.

1. Mix 1 cup white flour and remaining dry ingredients in medium bowl.
2. Warm milk, honey and oil in microwave in 2 cup measuring cup. Use high power for 45 seconds.
3. Add milk mixture to flour and stir to blend well.
4. Add remaining flour and drained dates (blot dates or raisins between paper towels to dry). Stir until forming soft dough, scraping sides of bowl.
5. Spray dough and sides of mixing bowl with Pam, shape dough in smooth ball.
6. Cover with plastic wrap and set in warm place to rise for one hour.
7. Punch down dough and divide in half.
8. Shape into oblong loaf for tall pots and roll dough out into rectangle shape and spread with margarine and sprinkle heavy with cinnamon and sugar. Roll up from the long side and pinch along seam to seal. Place dough in prepared large pot.
9. Use remaining dough and prepare as described above but cut in 1-inch slices and place in your low terra cotta pan. For both loaf and cinnamon rolls brush tops with margarine and sprinkle with cinnamon sugar.
10. Set in warm place for one hour, cover with plastic wrap.
11. Bake in oven preheated to 350 degrees for 20-30 minutes until brown.

Nothing compares to warm cinnamon toast and butter or fresh baked cinnamon rolls. If this all seems like a lot of work you will appreciate what these early women had to do for they're baking. Once you season your pots they will be ready for more baking of bread or rolls. If you really want to fudge on the work you can buy frozen bread at the grocery story but then it would not be a complete experience.

DRIED MEAT JERKY

Dried meat was a common staple for our ancestors on their long journeys either by caravans or by sea. Using the sun with spices to dry their jerky was a good source of protein on those long journeys. The following are recipes that one can use to marinate your meat and dry in your oven or in a food dehydrator. To prepare meat, cut off all fat then cut lean meat in long strips, then marinade in desired sauce. Place in refrigerator until ready to dry in oven. Drain and wipe off excess marinade with paper towels and dry in oven or dehydrator from 10 to 20 hours. I prefer beef so did not experiment with pork, chicken or turkey.

MY FAVORITE MARINADE
½-cup Soy Sauce1-clove garlic mashed
2-tablespoon onion finely diced
2-tablespoon honey or molasses

2-tablespoon tomato puree
½-cup Worcestershire Sauce
1-teaspoon salt
½-teaspoon cinnamon
½-teaspoon pepper
2-3-pounds of lean beef cut in strips.
Mix ingredients and marinate at least an hour. Place meat on a wire rack on a cookie sheet lined with foil place in oven to dry at 250 degrees. Bake in this slow oven until desired dryness is obtained. Turn strips often while drying.

SWEET-SOUR MARINADE

½-cup red wine vinegar or balsamic vinegar
½-cup brown sugar
1-teaspoon garlic powder
1-teaspoon onion powder
½-teaspoon cinnamon
¼-teaspoon ground ginger
1-teaspoon salt
½-cup Soy Sauce
½-cup Pineapple Juice
3-3 ½-pounds of lean beef cut in strips.
    Follow direction as stated above.

HOT AND SPICY MUSTARDS

    Mustard seeds have been found in India and China for many years and I found this fresh ground hot and spicy mustard a great way to spice up meats or on bread and crackers. Another way of using those beef Jerky strips dipped in fresh ground mustard. You may find the black mustard seeds in health food stores but yellow mustard seeds are available in most grocery stores. You can grind the seeds using a pestle, but I use a separate coffee grinder for this purpose only. This makes a finely ground spread that I store in decorative jars. They make great gifts too.

MUSTARD

2-ounces of black mustard seeds
2-ounces of yellow mustard seeds
4-fluid ounces of balsamic vinegar
1-clove garlic minced
¼-cup onion minced
½-teaspoon cinnamon
½-teaspoon red pepper flakes
½-teaspoon salt

Soak mustard seeds in vinegar using a plastic covered bowl for at least 24 hours. I use my mini-chopper to mince the garlic and onion and add to the mustard after soaking with cinnamon, red pepper flakes and salt. Place this mixture a small amount at a time in the coffee grinder, scraping sides and whirl off and on until desired smoothness. If you do not want to use the coffee grinder you can grind with a pestle or rolling pin but it sure takes longer.

Place in clean jars and cover tightly, store in cool dry area for a few weeks to age before using.

SWEET-SOUR MUSTARD

1-ounce yellow mustard seeds
¼-cup cider vinegar
1-clove garlic
¼-cup onion
1-teaspoon cinnamon/sugar
¼-teaspoon salt
1-teaspoon horseradish

I place all the above ingredients in my coffee grinder and it whips up just great and refrigerate. Store prepared mustard in covered container. Great with ham, roast beef, hamburgers or just about anything you want to try.

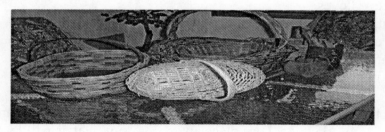

THE MANY USES OF CINNAMON

Potpourri or a mixture of dried flowers and spices has been in existence for generations. The love of this way of preserving flowers and bringing the sweet scents of spices to many homes is being repeated from one generation to another. You can choose what variety of flower you prefer but cinnamon is always a favorite to add to your mixture.

POTPOURRI AROMA

6-cups assorted dried flowers
1-cup Lavender
¼-cup Allspice
¼-cup Cloves
1-cup broken Cinnamon stick
½-cup dried Lemon and Orange peel
2-tablespoons of Orris root
10-drops of cinnamon oil

1. Pick fresh flowers and place petals on newspaper or paper towels in cool dry place away from sun. Petals will feel like tissue paper when dry. Some petals will take up to 10 days to dry. Store in covered containers until ready to mix potpourri.
2. Pare orange and lemon rind with vegetable peeler, omitting pulp. Dry on newspapers until crisp. (Suggestion the item listed in these two sections can be dried in your microware or a dehydrator-watch carefully.)
3. Crush cinnamon sticks and citrus peel with mallet.

4. Place all dry ingredients except oil in large container with tight fitting lid and shake gently to blend. Add oil and mix well by shaking gently.
5. Store in dark area for a few weeks, shaking gently every few days.
6. Fill potpourri in glass jars or place plastic wrap in bottom of baskets to contain your potpourri. To refresh scent add extra drops of cinnamon oil, stir gently to distribute oil.
7.

CANDLES MADE EASY

Here is an easy way to make candles for just a special purpose

with color you want to match your décor. Use a double boiler or another way is to clean a tin can medium size. Shave or cut candle wax or old candles into this can. If you are planning a special color add crayons to your wax to get the desired shade. Place your can in pan of simmering hot water. Stir the wax until all is melted. Remember the finished candles will be a lighter shade than the melted wax. After wax has melted you can add drops of essence of cinnamon, rose, lavender or any scent you prefer. Prepare containers either glass or ceramic and use purchase prepared wicks from a craft supply store. The wicks may have a weighted bottom to help keep the wick in center of finished candle. If using un-weighted wicks, anchor it to the center of your container with a few drops of melted wax. Lay a pencil across the container to hold your wick in place. When your wax is melted handle the tin of hot wax very carefully using hot mitt and slowly pour wax into your container. Let sit until firm and your candles will be ready for just the right place and scent.

Candle plaques are an added decorative touch. These are made by adding melted candle wax with essence oils into molds found in craft stores. To add the hanger lay, a ribbon or cord on back of partially set wax and cover with more melted wax. When completely set, remove from mold. Hang on mirror with suction cup hangers. Hang on the wall but would suggest gluing on a felt backing so it will not stain the walls.

COSMETICS OF THE AGES

We have read in many accounts of history that the use of cosmetics had been in existence during Egyptian and Roman times. The women of these days were concerned about their beauty; many royal courts and baths here are a few home made products you may want to experiment contained the use of special oils and fragrances. With these special oils it not only cleansed the skin, but also kept it moist and supple to prevent wrinkles. Even today with the abundance of cosmetics available with.

INFUSED OILS

Infused oils can be made at home. Start with dried flowers either roses or a variety of dried flowers. Fresh flowers may be used, but it may take longer as the accumulation of water will have to be siphoned off. Always use clean sterilized dry jar with a tight fitting lid. Pack your flowers well into the jar; pour a good grade of olive oil poking down the flowers to pack tightly. Place this covered jar in a cool dry place to infuse for 6 weeks. Check jar and fill to top with oil as needed. Place a label on jar so you remember just what flowers you are infusing. When time has lapsed, pour oils through cheesecloth into sterilized dry decorative bottle with stopper or cork. Let set for a few more days at room temperature, may be kept in refrigerator for longer storage. Thus, infused oils can be used as an ointment. Romans, Greeks and Egyptians women used this infused oils to enhance their beauty.

This same method of infusing can be used for dried whole spices, such as cinnamon, cloves, nutmeg, mace and ginger. Decant into decorative clean bottle and add a small cinnamon stick for decoration. These oils will make added spice to your bath water. Experiment with herbs and spices as a good choice for spicing up your salads and other foods plus they make great gifts in decorative bottles.

The information found here on the section of Cosmetics of the Ages was taken from the web site of (alternative.com) on beauty products in ancient times. Check out her web site for interesting beauty works. I included a portion of the recipes of antiquity for cold cream, lotions, ointments and wrinkle creams that are listed on this web site. If you can find these products listed you can experiment in the beauty products of Cleopatra or the Royal ladies of Rome. Here are a few examples.

ROSE COLD CREAM – Take 20mm Rosewater, 18 g. beeswax, l gr. Borax, 61 gr. Almond Oil, l ml Rose Oil. Melt wax and add oil. Dissolve borax in rosewater and bring to same temperature as the warmed oil and melted wax. Stir slowly the water solution into the oil/wax mixture, then add the rose and continue to stir with out ceasing.

PERSIAN BEAUTY BATH OF GRAINS – Take 3 lb. Pearl Barley, 3 lb. Powdered Lupuline, l lb. Rice, l lb. Borax, l lb. each Rosemary and Angelica. Boil all together in enough water to cover then add directly to bath.

POMATUMS AND WRINKLE CREAMS – Take ½ oz. Vegetable oil, 1 oz. of oil of tartar, ½ oz. of mucilage of quince, ¾ oz. of Caruys, 30 grains borax, plus 30 grains of sal gem. Stir all together with a wooden spoon till smooth. Apply as a mask and let dry then wash off.

A LOTION TO MAKE HAIR GROW: – Take the tops of hemp plants as soon as they sprout forth and infuse them for 24 hours in water. Dip the teeth of the hair comb in this solution and bush the hair back to front. It will certainly make the hair grow.

The best reformers are those that start…with themselves.   Letta ☺

THE CINNAMON STICK

Tales of the Spice Trade

PART 3

EXPLORATION AND PIRATES

EXPLORING THE PURSUIT OF SPICES

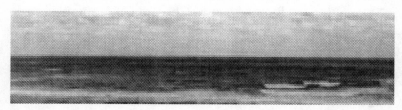

For centuries, legends of sea monsters, brought terror to sailors. The sailors were hindered from sailing too far from shore because they thought they would drop off the end of the ocean. The rage that spurred men on to explore the sea was the search for possible fortunes, adventure and the excitement of the unknown.

In the 1400's Europe entered the age of exploration. The world opened up to men with vision, such as Prince Henry, the Navigator of Portugal. He believed in exploration of the sea and founded a Naval Institute in 1418. His plan was to collect information on geographic findings in hopes of making new land discoveries. He attracted leading navigators, geographers and astronomers to study sea routes. His aim was to trace the source of all the rich imports, including cinnamon and cassia,  coming from the Far East. In 1471 this Naval College began to record facts of voyages taken south along the west coast of Africa. In 1486, Bartholemew Diaz sailed south along the west coast of Africa, passed the Cape of Good Hope and reported an open sea beyond. All these recordings prepared Portugal for further exploration.

News of these discoveries excited other explorers, such as Christopher Columbus, who believed he could reach the Far East by sailing directly west over the open ocean. It was believed that Columbus saw a world globe produced in 1492 by Martin Behain who was from Germany. This globe showed the world to be round and Japan only 3,000 miles due west from Europe. With this knowledge, Columbus approached Portugal with his idea of sailing west to reach the Far East but Portugal refused to sponsor his plan. After this rejection, Columbus went to Spain and received backing from King Ferdinand and Queen Isabella. Spain was turning to exploration to help enrich and enlarge their holdings. With this in mind Ferdinand and Isabella gave Columbus three ships named the Nina, Pinta and the Santa Maria. Columbus set sail on August 3, 1492 and after sailing for 33 days his calculation of 3,000 miles; he thought he should have reached the Far East. On October 12 he landed on an island, which he named San Salvador. He visited many islands in the area and called his discovery "The Indies." He still believed he found the Orient but was disappointed when he could not find the country of China.

While Columbus and his men from the three ships explored many islands, some of the men found what they thought were pieces of bark. This bark they found was called wild cinnamon, which we now call allspice. After this discovery, on March 15,

1493, Columbus returned to Spain where he received honors for his discoveries. Later, he returned to these new islands and set up a colony. He discovered that it was not the Far East, but a new very large great continent. Columbus was the first to bring Europe to this "New World", now called North and South America.

Portugal continued they're exploring when on July 1497 Vasco De Gama sailed from Lisbon. His journey took him along the west coast of Africa, around the southern tip and up the east coast of Africa. On this trip, he discovered beautiful cultured Arabian cities along the eastern coast. In the port of Mombasa he persuaded an Indian navigator to guide him across the Indian Ocean to India. In May 1, 1498 De Gama reached Calicut on the Malabar Coast of India. While at the markets the European crude hardware and rough cloth offered by De Gama was insulting to the Indian merchants. These merchants were used to trading for gold and silver for over 1000 years. While in Calicut, De Gama stayed in India for six months observing pepper and spices being traded in the markets. During his stay he observed the port filled with vessels from China, Arabia and India each with valuables merchandise for the busy market place.

Vasco De Gama's trip to India took two years to complete. He had sailed 24,000 miles returning to Portugal with only 55 of the 170 members of his crew. He arrived in Portugal with enough spices and information to motivate a return trip and a determination to force his way into the valuable spice trade. Portugal also was willing to sponsor a fleet of 15 ships in 1502 to capture the port of Calicut. European poorly made goods may have been crude, but their guns were superior. With revenge, he returned to India, attacking and capturing Calicut, for the insulting reception he received on his first trip.

De Gama established two trading posts along the Indian coast. When De Gama returned to Lisbon he impressed the government with cargos of spices, sacks of cinnamon, cassia, pepper, nutmeg, mace and cloves. In the next ten years Portugal took key ports along the Spice Route from India to Ceylon. In 1511 Portugal crossed the Bay of Bengal and took control of a group of the islands in Indonesia. These islands became known as the  Isle of Spices or "Spice Islands". The increased presence of Portugal in the Far East destroyed the monopoly of the Spice Route held by the Arab Countries for over 1000 years. The Arabs were shut out of the Spice trade again as it affected many of the countries along the Spice Route. These countries could not count on the exorbitant revenue they collected through taxes on spices passing through their country. Venice and Genoa soon heard the news of Portugal's triumphant voyages. The bankers and merchants reacted in shocked horror, as they realized their monopoly also was broken.

Another explorer, Ferdinand Magellan of Portugal, feeling he was not dutifully rewarded for the battles he won in East Indies from 1505 to 1513, he offered his services to Spain. They, in turn, offered him five ships and 280 men which allowed Magellan to set sail on September 25, 1519, taking a new direction around the southern tip of South America. When Magellan died after reaching the Philippines and claimed them for Spain, One of his ships with 18 men remaining continued around the tip of Africa and returned to Spain. When this ship reached Lisbon in 1522, they completed the first trip around the world. In spite of the heavy human losses, this expedition was considered a financial success. Spain had used the silver from Mexico to help generate trade along the Spice Route. The riches they brought back to Spain were 26 tons of cloves, sacks of nutmeg, cinnamon and cassia, which covered the cost of the trip.

The Portuguese regime in the Spice Islands was filled with violence, plunder and oppression of the natives. The cinnamon forests were exploited with the natives used as slaves to harvest the cinnamon bark. The Portuguese shipped 250,000 pounds of cinnamon bark from their ports annually, and resold it in European markets. They jealously guarded their secret of navigation and monopolized the trade that expanded the spice supply in Europe for 100 years.

Soon ambitious merchants in other countries challenged Portugal's trade in the Far East. They also disregarded the dangers that were found on the open sea and were willing to wage war for the trade of spices.

DEATH AND DESTRUCTION ON THE SPICE ROUTE

Ambition and greed contributed to an atmosphere of lunacy. In its desire for profit and power, no nation considered the waste of human lives a problem. Human life was secondary to the benefits of trade and wealth. Spain and Portugal held on to their power throughout the 1500's. In 1494, these two powers made an agreement to divide the world. They drew up a treaty on an imaginary line and called it "Line of Demarcation." This showed that Spain would control the West and Portugal the East. When other European nations became envious of their monopoly, they worked to increase their knowledge of the sea as the interest in trade exploded all over Europe.

 An amazing development occurred in the waters near Portugal in 1592, when six small English warships captured a Portuguese merchant ship returning from India. The English were in awe at the size of this vessel with a 1,600-ton capacity. It was far bigger than any English ship and was covered with gilded wood and painted decoration. The cargo carried chests

of gold and silver coins, tons of pepper, cloves, cinnamon, nutmeg and mace, along with diamonds, pearls and exotic far eastern fabrics. It so impressed the English that they formed a company called "The British East India Company" and frantically began building bigger ships.

Meanwhile, in March of 1594, the Netherlands set up "Dutch East India Company" to finance voyages to the Orient for spices. The Dutch had superior ships because for many years they had carried on trade along the European Coastline. In their pursuit to establish trade with the Orient they used Jewish merchants who had experience with Asian trade and could also help finance such overseas ventures. In the spring of 1595, four Dutch ships left for the East and returned to Amsterdam two and a half years later with precious cargo. They brought back 295 bags of pepper, 45 tons of cinnamon, cassia, and nutmeg, with 30 bales of mace. It more than covered the cost of the trip and also established a trade agreement with the island of Java. It was recorded that the 249 men who left on this trip, only 89 returned. Many men on these trips died from many causes including shipwrecks and poor living conditions.

Sea travel was dangerous but countries were willing to take the risks of the unknown. Crews for the ships were rounded up as if they were herds of cattle, consisting of drunkards, derelicts and slum dwellers that were used as common hands. Life aboard ship was harsh, with strict discipline to keep the sailors in line. When they showed resistance they were beaten or hung. Seasickness was widespread, and the heat along the Equator was unbearable. Even with these hardships, the promise of wealth and exciting sea travel to exotic places lured these young men to sign up. The crew's living quarters deep within the ship were cramped and miserable with odors and numerous rodents. Ventilation was poor and oxygen so short that a candle would not burn. Sickness, such as malnutrition, scurvy, dehydration, malaria, cholera and typhoid, were common. People cared little for cleanliness and their clothes swarmed with lice. Infectious diseases passed quickly from one man to another. The crew's meals were hardly palatable; which were eaten from wooden bowls and they sat wherever they could find a place. The water aboard ship became stagnant and rats and cockroaches infected the food supply.

The skilled hands such as the captain, boatswain, gunners, cooks, merchants, doctor and priest had more favorable quarters. They regarded themselves as gentlemen and lived in comfortable large cabins apart from the crew. They had better food, dined in a dining room with white linen tablecloths. Their food and drink was in quantity and well seasoned with three hot meals a day.

An average journey of these trading ships took two to three years. The amount of food these ships had to carry was enormous. The ships were loaded with live animals such as chickens, pigs and goats with barrels of pickled vegetables, potatoes, water and rum. With a ship loaded with gunpowder, the threat of fire held the most terror, as candles were used for lighting, stoves for cooking, a  blacksmith's forge, and sailors who smoked pipes, all was a threat.

With all these risks, ambition and greed encouraged the Europeans nations to further their search for wealth in the spice trade. The Government was not concerned with the dangers at sea, as long as there were courageous men to take the risks. In 1602, the Dutch sent an enormous fighting fleet to the Spice Islands. The Portuguese were stretched thin trying to control all their holdings and were unable to keep out intruders. The Dutch were able to grab a share of the Asian spice trade. In 1612 the British succeeded in conquering most of the Indian ports along the Spice Route.

Confrontations between the nations continued because Portugal did not want to give up control of the spice trade, which they had dominated for years. They continued to battle with the Dutch and English ships loaded with spices. These activities irritated the Indian Mogul, ruler of India that he started to help the British defeat the Portuguese in 1615. By 1621, the Dutch had set up trade agreements with rulers of the Spice Islands. These actions now allowed the English and Dutch to control of the Spice Trade.

In 1652, with the many ships sailing back and forth between Europe and the Far East the Dutch established a settlement at the Cape of Good Hope called "Cape town" located on the southern tip of Africa. It was set up by the Dutch East India Company and was a halfway stop in the difficult voyage from Europe to the Spice Islands. In this settlement, homes were built for lodging, gardens and orchards were planted and domesticated animals were available for fresh meat. Sometimes ships stayed for months to heal their sick and restore their provisions. This was one event, in the years of the death and destruction on the Spice Route that saved lives.

Even though Portugal was gone from the Spice Route, ambition and greed remained and the battles continued. The European rivals preyed on each other and all was fair game for the pirates. Although pirates had been on the sea since the first boat set sail, the Spice Route now saw a new enemy, the "Yankee Pirates".

FREEBOOTERS-THE YANKEE PIRATES

After Columbus discovered the New World, it did not take long for European business to set up colonies in America. The so-called "Line of Demarcation", proclaimed by Portugal and Spain, was ignored by other European nations. Impressed by the new-armed World's wealth, multitude of explorers there clamored to claim new discoveries. Wherever there were numerous ships, one would always find pirates. It wasn't until the discovery of America that piracy became a big business.

There were armed men who preferred to steal rather than earn an honest living. Ashore, they were called robbers or highwaymen, but on the high seas they were called pirates, freebooters or buccaneers.

During the late 1600's, the Spanish galleons, loaded with gold and silver bullion, were making numerous trips from Mexico and to Spain. News of these richly loaded ships brought the pirates to the waters off the Mexican shores. They preyed on these large sailing vessels and then fled to hide in the Caribbean Islands. It is estimated the pirates took hundreds of millions of dollars worth of bullions from these raids. In the early 1700's, Spain strengthened its naval forces and the pirates began to look for new spoils. They found a suitable spot near the Red Sea and Indian Ocean on the western section of the Spice Route, a suitable spot. Pirates preferred trade routes that passed through islands and harbors because they could hide and find places to sell their stolen treasures.

Even though the pirates had little education and many could not read or write but they were experts at fighting, seamanship and geography. They exchanged information relating to trade routes and coastal ports that were not defended. The British East India Company and the Dutch East India Company joined forces to defend the spice routes from the Yankee Pirates. These European Trade Companies carried an abundance of wealth along the trade routes and needed to protect themselves from this new danger.

The area that was the most dangerous was in the Indian Ocean. It started at the top of the inlet to the Red Sea and sailing south to Madagascar then east to the Malabar Coast of India and back to the Red Sea. Within this area, the pirates found numerous hiding places in the natural harbors and inlets of the many islands especially Madagascar. This large island was considered the headquarters for the pirates. After the pirates stripped a ship of its cargo, they would flee to the safety of Madagascar's many ports.

Captain Avery was most responsible for spreading the word about the riches to be taken in the Red Sea and Indian Ocean. He captured a rich vessel, laden with a lavish cargo, in route to the Red Sea for a pilgrimage to Mecca in Arabia. The ship was loaded with gold, silver, rare spices and jewels to be offered to the shrine in Mecca. Captain Avery looted everything of value from this ship including rich clothing, goblets of gold and silver and great sums of money. The cargo was estimated to be worth several million dollars. The news of this looting received great coverage in newspapers, which created fame for Avery and his crew. This news sent hundreds of pirates to the Red Sea looking for quick and easy wealth.

Pirate ships varied in size. They ranged from small sloops to schooners and frigates. Usually they were smaller than their prey because speed and maneuverability was important for making a fast getaway. The process of boarding a vessel was usually the same. They never ran broadside because this was where the cannons were located. They chose to board at the rear of the ship and engage in hand-to-hand fighting. Weapons of choice were pistols, knives, cutlasses, sabers, boarding axes and pikes. Disposing of their loot was fairly easy. Gold and silver coins and gold dust and bars were traded in port, along India and

Africa. The jewels, spices, ivory, jade and textiles were taken to the American colonies and sold to local merchants.

Colonial America was still under British rule and was restricted from foreign trade. The American Colonists were forced to trade  only with England, often at high prices for poor quality. They were restrained from purchasing luxury items from France, Spain or the Netherlands. This included spices, wines, olive oil, cloth, shoes and jewelry. Inevitably, smuggling became a thriving business with the pirates who arrived with rich silks, spices, gems and other luxury items. The American merchants yielded to temptations and bought these looted goods. Many colonial families, including Quakers, made their fortune from looted treasures taken in the Red Sea. For years, the merchants along the Atlantic Coast, particularly from Massachusetts to South Carolina, became wealthy on Spice Route merchandise.

The most publicized pirate and the one who may have caused the downfall of the piracy business, was Captain Kidd. He was allegedly hired by British and American merchants in hopes to rid the Red Sea of pirates. It is unclear if this was a plan to gain wealth on the spoils, or a legal war to stop pirating. During Captain Kidd's venture into the Red Sea, he captured a great vessel, weighing 400 tons, from an Armenian merchant. It held the richest cargo ever taken and surpassed Captain Avery's loot. Captain Kidd must have decided or was urged by his crew to divide the cargo amongst them. He released the passengers and crew of the ship on the coast of India and then fled to America.

Captain Kidd landed on Gardiner Island owned by John Gardiner, now called Long Island, New York. Kidd previously received permission from Gardiner to bury chests of merchandise on this island. In these chests he claimed to have bolts of silks, muslin and calico, gold cloth and bushels of cloves and nutmeg, which he purchased in Madagascar. He also secretly sent treasures to friends for safekeeping. When Captain Kidd went ashore, he was arrested and jailed after being  given a promise that he would receive an English pardon. Governor Bellomont of New York wanted Kidd found guilty of pirating, even though he also may have helped finance Kidd's trip to the Red Sea. Colonist Bellomont was not authorized to hold a trial, so Kidd was transferred to England. After this trial he was found guilty of piracy and was hung in chains, in public view over the Thames River, in an effort to discourage future piracy.

The fate of Captain Kidd did curtail pirating in the Red Sea area, but America had profited from spices even if it was in an illegal way. The sudden wealth that poured into the Colonies had a powerful effect on the economy, politics and moral standards. Strict British rule and heavy taxation led to unrest and brought about an uprising of the American settlers. The Revolutionary War also known as the "American War of Independence" was won, by using the wealth gained from smuggled goods. This wealth gave Colonial settlers the strength to rebel against the British power. The French aided the Colonist efforts and America received its independence on July 4, 1776. This conflict gave America freedom to set up trade with other nations. In the following years America became strong in global markets, which helped the country prosper and expanded the spice trade.

DAILY LIFE ON THE OPEN SEAS

There are four items, which were referred to in the Bible and now plentiful today. All four of these items would have been in use during the period of the times of exploration and piracy upon the high seas. These four are; vinegar, oils, honey and garlic this section covers items from all four. Following are suggestions that may have been used on the sailing ships in these early times.

VINEGAR

Vinegar was discovered when some foods turned into wine then after further fermentation, turned into vinegar. It was first introduced as a medicine, and then as a preservative for foods. Vinegar has numerous uses from cleansing items, cures for many ailments, preserving foods, and cosmetic use.

SPICED PICKLED EGGS

12-eggs, hard-cooked and peeled
1 small onion, thinly sliced
2-minced clove of garlic
3-cups cider vinegar
1-small cinnamon sticks
1-tablespoon honey
1-teaspoon whole allspice
1-teaspoon whole cloves
½-teaspoon whole coriander seeds
1-small slice fresh ginger

Place eggs, onion and garlic in a wide mouth jar with close fitting lid. Combine remaining ingredients in a non-metallic pan and bring to a boil, reduce heat and simmer for 5 minutes. Pour over eggs mixture, cover and store in refrigerator for a week to blend flavors. Will keep for over a month, you can replace fresh boiled hard boiled eggs making sure they reach the bottom layer.

OILS

Oil is another common item today and was also used in the earliest times. Olive Oil has been a favorite of good cooks everywhere. Oils were used for many purposes aboard ship such as cooking oils and lamp oils. It was used for cleaning and preserving the wood on the ship and keeping the cooking utensils from rusting.

SPICED OIL
1-pint Olive Oil
1-tablespoon coriander seeds
1-tablespoon crushed cinnamon sticks
1-tablespoon cloves

Lightly crush the coriander and cloves, place in jar with crushed cinnamon sticks in a bottle with stopper or cork. Pour olive oil over the spices seal and shake gently to distribute spices. Keep for a week, shaking bottle occasionally. Strain into another bottle and store in a cool, dark place, use as a flavoring for dressings on salads and fruits.

HONEY

Honey is a sweetener available from the beginning of time. Often mentioned in the Bible, it was prized as the food from the Gods. One can imagine that this sweetener was used on those long ocean voyages. Honey is another product that has many uses from remedies of all kinds to making delicious foods.

HONEY CORN BREAD

1-cup sifted flour
3-teaspoon baking powder

1-teaspoon salt
1-cup yellow corn meal
2-tablespoon wheat germ
1-egg slightly beaten
1-cup milk
¼-cup melted butter3-tablespoon honey.

Mix flour, baking powder and salt. Add corn meal and wheat germ. Combine egg, milk, butter and honey. Pour into flour mixture and stir until just moistened. Pour into butter 8x8 square pan, bake in 350-degree oven for about 20-25 minutes. Cool on wire rack and cut in serving size and spread with Honey Cinnamon Butter

HONEY CINNAMON BUTTER

½-pound butter or margarine
2-tablespoon honey
1-teaspoon ground cinnamon

Let butter or margarine stand at room temperature to soften. Add honey and cinnamon and stir until well blended. Place in a covered jar with lid and store in refrigerator, it goes well with toast, muffins or cinnamon bread as pictured.

GARLIC

Garlic, another food that has been around the world and back still produces many uses for our good health. Egyptians, Romans and Greek have mentioned these little bulbs of garlic in early writings for its many healing powers. Garlic is available in pill form, syrups, tea and gargle or just fresh cooked in a variety of foods.

GARLIC ROASTED MEAT

3-4-pound roast beef
3-large cloves of garlic
2-tablespoon spice rubs (instruction below)

Peal garlic and cut into long thin strips. Make slits into the roast beef with a sharp knife and poke garlic slivers into the slit. Place these slits on both sides of beef using all your garlic slivers. Using one tablespoon of spice rub, rub into one side and repeat other side of beef. Place roast on rack over drip pan and bake at 350 degrees use meat thermometer for correct doneness.

SPICE RUB

1-tablespoon ground black pepper
¼-teaspoon ground red pepper
½-teaspoon white pepper
½-teaspoon ground nutmeg
½-teaspoon ground cumin
½-teaspoon salt
½-teaspoon garlic powder
½-teaspoon brown sugar

Blend all ingredients in a jar with lid and shake to mix well. Use as desired to rub on meats before baking or grilling.

BEAUTY IS ALL AROUND US

People of all races and civilizations were concerned about how they looked and how they decorated their living quarters. In earliest civilizations many women loved to pamper themselves and to decorate their homes. Here are a few suggestions as to what can be tried to better understand how people, in days gone by, had to do to accomplish their desire for beauty.

BEAUTY FOR THE BATH

BATH SALTS

1-small box Epson Salts
5-10 drops of essence oil of cinnamon
Food Coloring

Place Epson Salts in large bowl and add essence of cinnamon oil. Separate salts in several small bowls and add a variety of food coloring to match your bathroom colors. Alternate layers of salts in a jar with a close fitting lid and place in bathroom. Use several scoops of salts to your bath water and enjoy the soothing salts and aroma.

SOAP BALLS

Shave left over soap plus lotion soap such as Ivory
4-5-drops of essence of cinnamon or lavender oils

Place shaved soap in amount you wish to experiment with in top of double boiler or place a clean can in pan of boiling water and melt soap. Place drops of oil in melted soap and pour into low dish covered with saran wrap. When soap is cooled form into balls and place in a container on your bathroom counter.

SIMMERING OIL
1-cup sweet almond or peanut oil
6-tablespoon rose-petals
5-6 drops of essence oils

Bend ingredients well. And store in small jar. Pour in simmer pot with small candle and enjoy the aroma in your bathroom.

EGYPTIAN FACIAL MASK

1-teaspoon honey
1-egg white
1-teaspoon milk
¼-teaspoon cinnamon

Beat all ingredients together until well mixed. Spread over clean face and neck omitting around eyes area. Leave on for ½ hour or until it feels dry and tight. Wash off with lukewarm water, splash on cold water and blot dry with soft towel

BEAUTY FOR THE HOME

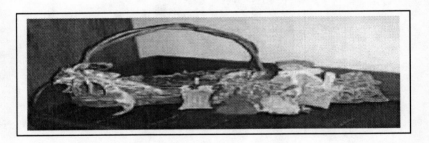

CINNAMON POTPOURRI FOR SACHETS

6-cups rose petals or assorted dried flowers-crushed
1-cups dried Rosemary
1-cup dried sweet marjoram
1-cup dried sweet basil
1-cup coriander seed
1-cup crushed cinnamon sticks
½-cup cloves
½-cup allspice
2-tablespoon orris root

8-10 drops of cinnamon oil

   In large bowl or pan stir all ingredients (except cinnamon oil) and mix well. Place drops of cinnamon oil and shake or toss to blend in oil. Place in lined baskets or place in sachet bags, direction given below.

SACHET BAGS

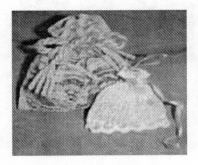

Two pieces of plain soft cloth-8-inches square
Matching thread
6-inches of ribbon

   Fold cloth in half, sew by hand or machine ¼-inch along bottom and one side. Fold down open end for two inches and stitch, turn bag inside out. This will make a sachet bag 4 by 6 inches. Fill bag with cinnamon dried flowers close to top, take ribbon and fold ribbon in half. Wrap the ribbon around bag and tie shut. Experiment with different size pieces of cloth adding lace for decoration and twisted rope for ribbon.

.

Where there is no vision,
…..progress falters.
Letta ☺

THE CINNAMON STICK

Tales of the Spice Trade

PART 4

AMERICA ENTERS THE SPICE TRADE

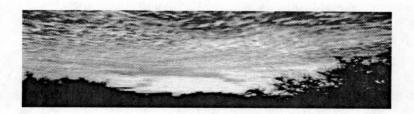

THE AMERICAN SPICE TRADE

America entered the latter years of the 1700's as a free nation. Freedom from British taxation and tyranny gave enterprising merchants and seamen an opportunity to expand their trade. As Independence became a reality, vessels belonging to United States merchants, had to make their way into areas, barred by England. This large region included India and the Far East markets.

European powers wished to retain their monopoly on products from this area. There was only one exception, the Chinese port of Canton, which was open to all trade. Chinese merchants were free to deal with any foreign ship and new traders were welcome. Americas' problem was to find a product to trade that would bring a high profit. The answer came from an American seaman named John Ledyard. He went to England and joined Captain Johnathan Cook on trips to the Far East. On these trips he observed Cook trading fur pelts to the Chinese for $100.00 each. Ledyard believed this was the key to launch American merchants into the trading for luxury goods.

In 1783, Robert Morris, of Philadelphia, took John Ledyard's information and promptly arranged with a group of merchants to help finance a trade experiment. When their first ship reached Canton in 1784, the American trade with China began. The Americans were amazed at what they saw, with the array of shipping vessels, exotic flotillas, barges, ferry boats, flower and food boats, gaily painted junks, sampans housing whole families, plus foreign merchant's ships of all sizes. All merchants handled their business through the Chinese trading posts, which were regulated by the Emperor of China. After trading, the American merchants returned 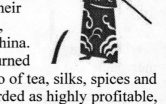 to New York on May 11, 1785 with a cargo of tea, silks, spices and chinaware. This first voyage was not regarded as highly profitable, but good enough to encourage more trips into the China trade.

The Chinese trade with America flourished as trade flowed back and forth across the sea. They brought exotic treasures to New York and Boston but it made its strongest effect on the little town of Salem, Massachusetts. The wharf in Salem harbor was the starting and ending  of world voyages. Along the wharf lay ships returning with tea and spices from China, coffee from Arabia, cotton goods from India, sisal from Manila and ivory and gold from Guinea. Salem Massachusetts was considered the main harbor for large volumes of trading from countries all over the world

The most important event was the

capture of the world pepper business from the Dutch, who had controlled the market for 100 years. The Americans mysteriously changed the flow of the pepper trade. According to a newspaper article, on April 15, 1788, Captain Carnes of Salem sailed into the China Sea and returned with his ship loaded with cassia, cinnamon, camphor, gold dust and pepper. He refused to reveal how he acquired the pepper and then after another trip to the China Seas he returned to Salem with his ship laden with peppercorn shoveled in like gravel. On Captain Carnes third trip, he returned in October 1799 with 79 tons of pepper worth $100,000.00. By this time, it was discovered he was trading with the natives of Sumatra, an island of the Spice Islands, who were eager to double cross the Dutch. The Dutch had mistreated the natives and they were eager to trade for the silver offered by the Americans. Spice trading was a rough business, with underhanded dealings and faulty scales, making the merchants to be on alert. The smuggling of pepper and overproduction of cinnamon soon forced the Dutch East India Company into bankruptcy.

American seamen in Salem had a sense of their place in history when they organized the East India Marine Society. This organization was open to all seamen, who, according to their rules,  "actually navigated the sea, beyond the Cape of Good Hope and Cape Horn". They started a museum of items found on their voyages plus information and maps on the routes they traveled. This collection remains in the East India Marine Hall built in 1824, that Salem's true boundaries were the seaports of the world. The city of Salem had on its seal, the motto, "To the fartherest port of the rich east".

In 1834 Harriet Martineau, an English author, wrote about her view of Salem, stating that it was a remarkable place. Salem had a population, at that time, of 14,000 and more wealth in proportions to any town in the world. It is told that a captain would put his older children in a boarding school, taking his wife and younger children on voyages around the world. He would return home with his ship loaded with merchandise of the highest value, plus prized possessions for the  family. This type of travel was not an unusual occurrence as it was the way things were in the late 1800's for the people of Salem.

With the overproduction of spices in the Far East, it caused spices to become an inexpensive product. It did not mean it was not desired because people still craved the taste and smell of cinnamon and cassia. The buying and selling of spices was big business. With the increase in population, more people were in the market for these same spices. The passion and pursuit of cinnamon and cassia was not the rage as before but it turned into one of the world's everyday enjoyments.

DECLINE OF THE SPICE RAGE

The decline of the spice rage occurred after a group of unrelated events in the 1800's. These events included the corruption of the east India Company with the cost of waging wars in foreign lands, the opening of the Suez Canal and the expansion of spice production. Other changes in the world were also taking place, such as better education was leading to social change and the economies of countries were leveling out. No single country held control over vast territories. The world was becoming more civilized and progressive, but sadly not free from corruption, greed and destruction.

The British East India Company developed into the most powerful private commercial organization the world had ever known. It had the status of a semi-government. It commanded military forces, acquired and administered territories and minted its own money. Such authority over a realm as vast as India, by a private organization, was on oddity that lasted 260 years.

The men who went to India had only one aim in mind, to get rich quick. Elihu Yale is one example of English Officers who acquired riches while in service in India. He was 23 years old when he went to work in India for the British East India Company, starting as a minor official. He later became Governor of Fort Saint George in Madras and returned to England a wealthy man after 22 years of service with a valuable collection of East Indian artifacts.

On the suggestion of Cotton Mather, an American Puritan, he asked Elihu Yale to donate a large part of his collection to the Collegiate School of Connecticut. After this donation, the name of the institution was change to the Yale University. How Yale acquired his wealth was never questioned. It was common knowledge that many British officers gathered their wealth in the trading of spices and exotic goods while serving in India. The opportunity for fraud, embezzlement, and illicit dealings was always present in trade dealings.

In 1813, the British House of Commons voted to halt the East India Company's monopoly on the Far East trade. They opened Eastern trade to other English merchants. When the British and the Dutch signed a treaty in 1824 a relative calm overtook the Spice Route. This was a welcome pause in the intense struggle for supremacy in the Far East.

At this time nations gave permission to officers and sailors to trade on their own. Everyone was allotted space according to rank but everyone abused this practice. Goods were smuggled aboard the ship leaving little room for the company's cargo. Vast fortunes were made in a short time as men used every illegal means to acquire wealth.

In 1833, the English Parliament ordered the East India Company to cease all trade because of mismanagement and illegal activities, which threw the company into total chaos. The cost of waging wars to protect their holdings proved their undoing. In 1874 the British Government assumed control of the East India Company and it was dissolved. Because of these events trading of private companies were placed under the control of the government.

The most advanced idea for the Spice Route came in the 1800's when a plan was proposed for a canal between the Mediterranean Sea to the Red Sea. British Lt. Thomas Waghorn pioneered the plan. In 1869, Ferdinand de Lesseps of France built the canal, covering 100 miles from Port Said through the Isthmus of Suez to Port of Suez on the Red Sea. The canal, taking ten years to complete, was a relatively straight cut with no locks and few curves. At the narrowest part it was 150 feet wide but at other locations it was wide enough for ships to pass each other. This canal route, from London to Bombay, India, would take only 40 days. Previous trips around the Cape of Good Hope took from six months to a year.

With the opening of the Suez Canal, Spice Route, through the Red Sea, once again became the dominant long distance trading route. The speed of travel brought massive goods from one area to the other. Countries expanded their production of manufactured and agricultural product to use for expanded trading. The Dutch extended their cultivation of cinnamon plantations, along with their control of the pepper market, which caused them to be diligent in protection of this trade. India was still the central stopping place for ships making the trip to the Far East.

Spice plants were introduced into many tropical countries with the cultivation of these plants, helped produce a large amount of spices. Cloves, nutmeg, and mace were planted in more islands of Indonesia. The French introduced cinnamon, cassia, cloves and nutmeg into the Seychelles Islands along the east coast of Africa. The islands are now known for the wonderful aroma of spices that prevail everywhere. The expanded agricultural production and development extended into Madagascar, Philippines, Malaya, East Africa and India. This increase in the production of spices, coupled with the speed of transportation, helped bring about the decline of the spice rage in Europe. Supply was now catching up with demand. As extensive wealth from spices declined, Europeans countries still retained their control of the Far East and the spice trade. The spice rage continued in America as this new country was growing rapidly and substantial trade was needed to supply the hungry society.

SPICES ENTERS THE 20TH CENTURY

As the great riches of China and the Far East decreased, news of gold in California in the late 1840's and the Homestead Act in 1862 sent many people to seek their fortune in new places. Waves of immigrants flocked to America to begin new lives, people on foot, in covered wagons and on trains, began to settle the New World.

As the country became settled, trading for goods again became necessary. Farmers bartered for what they needed. With more population, peddlers appeared with packs of goods on their backs. Later, they carried goods in wagons pulled by horses, stopping wherever they found settlements. The peddlers worked the canal routes and the well-traveled roads. They carried such things as needles, pins, buttons, cloth, tin ware, patent medicines and nonperishable cooking supplies such as pepper, salt and spices.

Peddling supplies in the New World led to the opening of the general store. These were located where groups of people lived together. The stores were usually located in the center of towns. They were built as long buildings with a porch and hitching post out front. Flour, crackers, pickles and salt were stored in barrels, while other items were placed on shelves along the walls. In the middle of the store stood a large pot-bellied stove surrounded by 3 or 4 chairs that were placed so townspeople could gather to exchange news of the day. The store also housed a post office with numbered boxes for the people living in the area.

The storekeeper and his family sometimes lived on the second floor, which was handy when customers would need supplies. Many times merchandise was exchanged for locally grown produce but some items demanded a cash sale, such as coffee, spices and gunpowder because these items were in short supply.

Spice companies were formed to distribute the spices in America. The first company was started when two teenage brothers from Chelsa, Massachusetts, using their father's gristmill, ground a barrel of cinnamon bark. They then sold this ground cinnamon to Samuel Pierce's grocery store in Boston. Previously, cinnamon, pepper and other spices had to be ground by the homemaker using a pestle and mortar.

Spice Companies in business today such as Tone Brothers Inc. of Ankeny, Iowa and McCormick & Company Inc. of Hunt Valley, Maryland were founded in the 1800's. In 1783 Jehiel and I. E. Tone from Des Moines, Iowa started the Tone Brothers as a coffee and spice business. They employed 11 people and sold coffee and seven spices such as pepper, cinnamon, nutmeg, cloves, allspice, mace and ginger. They were sold to store, in bulk and resold to homemakers in small cans or containers.

McCormick & Company was started in a one-room cellar in Baltimore, Maryland by 25-year-old Willoughby M. McCormick. He, with his staff, two girls and a boy, first offered products such as root beer, flavoring extract, fruit syrup's and juices and sold these items door to door. In 1896, he bought the F. G. Emment Spice Company of Philadelphia and entered the spice field. In 1947, he acquired the A. Schilling & Company of San Francisco and thereby coast-to-coast distribution.

The American Spice Trade Association was formed in 1907 to help control the business practice, improve services to the public and promote new businesses. Membership was open to jobbers, manufacturers, wholesalers and retailers. Information was available to help them in their distribution and practices of the spice trade. Today, New York is the center of the spice trade. Each year over 500 ships bring spices to the United States ports for distribution to countries around the world.

For centuries, there were controversies concerning the differences between cassia and cinnamon. The United States uses more cassia, as Americans prefer the stronger flavor and darker color. Most of the true cinnamon imported into the United States is re-exported to Mexico and England. In 1938, the Food and Drug Administration gave official permission for the term cinnamon to be used for all cassia sold in America. So, when you sprinkle your toast with cinnamon and sugar it is really cassia.

Another area in which spices had a strong influence was in the aromatic interests of health and wellness. America was preoccupied with hygiene perhaps it was because we believed that cleanliness was next to godliness. Cleanliness was also a concern of the early Egyptian, Romans, Greeks and Arabs. Much was written about the early Roman baths but not much has been written about the Arabs. They had access to large amounts of spices; some of which were used in creating a sauna like bath in the desert. By spreading their robes over a pit in the ground they were able to clean their body and their clothes. They also put these aromatics between the folds of fabrics to keep them free of insects. The use of potpourri adapted from the Greeks, appeared in Colonial and Victorian times. Today there is a renewed interest in potpourri with burning pots of fragrant oils, scented candles, sachets, bath oils, shampoos and deodorants. Many of these items can be made at home but are available most everywhere at nominal costs.

People today, are becoming more health conscious and more interested in naturally grown foods and enhanced with the use of herbs and spices for flavor. Americans are concerned with the many preservatives and additives of manufactured goods. Spices for cooking are abundant in our grocery and specialty stores. Today you will find salt and pepper on most tables. In almost every nation the most widely used spice is Pepper. The United States is the largest consumer of pepper, followed by India, Russia, Germany, France and England. Cinnamon is widely used in many ways and is one of the main spices found in most kitchens.

 The old Spice Route is still well traveled and one will find ships of all sizes, some huge commercial ships still carrying cinnamon along with oil tankers, warships, personal yachts and tourist cruise ships. There are even guided tours of the Silk Route traveled by Marco Polo by just checking the Internet. Although much of this area was under strife during the early years of the Spice Trade, even today there is still find unrest in parts of these same areas.

The importance of the Arabs in the world has come full circle in the 21st Century, from their monopoly of the spices for 1,000 years, to their current control of oil. This product is making them wealthier than spices ever could. The Arabs still are in disagreement with each other and with the establishment of a Jewish state of Israel in 1945. This has left this area of the Mediterranean in a state of unrest for over 50 years. The world's dependence on oil has left this situation in a state of turmoil.

Ships have sailed over the seas caravans traveled over land people have met, mingled, shaken hands with one another and exchanged new ideas. Nations collected the riches and knowledge and passed them on to today's cultures. Wars cannot be overlooked or condoned, but wars continue to be a possibility into the 21st Century. Corruption and greed has gone on for centuries. It seems that we never learn from our past mistakes, since the same mistakes continue to occur.

Today, spices have developed a variety of new ways to enjoy food and fragrances. They have become less a necessity and more a pleasure in the art of living. Enjoy cinnamon and cassia because they have traveled a long and interesting journey to our homes. Savoring that next breakfast cinnamon roll and smell its sweet scent, then think of the great journey it took to get to your table.

CINNAMON ENTERS THE 21ST CENTURY

Today with all the new technology that is available businesses are temping the public to purchase new products. Kitchens are over flowing with all these new appliances that are thought to make ones work easier or the food tastier. Buyers are inundated with ads for fancy grills and smokers, from fast cooking microwaves, to food processors and other items to numerous to mention. One thing I thought I could not live without was a dehydrator for drying my own fruits, vegetables and herbs. Ever so often I get that urge to dry things especially in the summer with all those wonderful fruits and vegetables. See recipe below for Fruit Trail Mix not just for hikes but for snacks any time.

DEHYDRATOR DRIED FRUITS

I have a favorite such as apples, bananas, nectarines, plums, cantaloupes, and apricots. I found raisins and cranberries are not worth the effort as they are so reasonable to buy already dried. Turn the dehydrator on so it will warm up before putting in fruit. Peal and core apples, remove pits from other fruit, take slices of cantaloupe and remove rind and cut thin slices. I slice all fruits fairly thin except bananas slice ½ inch. Place them all in lemon water to soak for brief time. Place the fruit on towels to drain and blot with paper towels. I place the fruit on a cookie sheet covered with foil and sprinkled with cinnamon and sugar. Lay the fruit slices close together on the cookie sheet and sprinkle more cinnamon sugar on top of fruit. Place slices on dehydrator tray do not overlap fruit. Continue with fruit in as many trays as needed, close lid and let dehydrator run for at least 10-24 hours. Remove fruit from trays that have dried and arrange remaining slices around trays. You can dry fruit slices in your oven on racks at 200 degrees.

DRIED FRUIT TRAIL MIX

1-cup dried apples
1-cup dried banana slices
1-cup dried nectarine slices
1-cup dried plums\
1-cup dried apricots
1-cup dried cantaloupe
1-cup dried cranberries
1-cup raisins
1-cup flaked coconut
1-can mixed nuts

Place all ingredients in a large mixing bowl and stir with wooden spoon to mix all fruits and nuts until blended. Place in large mouth jars and seal. Place in small plastic bags for going on hikes but also good just eating out of the jar.

CINNAMON CARMEL CORN

A good suggestion when making this recipe is to prepare all equipment ahead of time. You will need two large pans, the size of a roaster, spray these with oil spray and divide into them 12-14 cups of popped pop corn. Using one can of mixed nuts divide the can of nuts into the two pans of popped corn. Prepare two large cookie sheets or broiler pans lining them with heavy foil, crimping the foils around the edges of pans. Spray each pan with oil spray.

The pan for cooking the Carmel mixture, use a two quart heavy pan or at least one with Teflon coating. I use wooden spoons or spatulas, or Teflon coated to stir the syrup while boiling. This makes a large amount of Cinnamon Carmel Corn and I store it in several glass jars as the pictures shows. Follow the directions for the recipe below.

2-sticks of margarine
2-cups brown sugar
½-cup white syrup or honey

Place margarine in sauce pan to melt, add brown sugar and syrup or honey. Stir constantly until sugar melts and begins to boil. Boil for five minutes continue to stir to keep mixture from boiling over. Remove from heat and add the following.

½-teaspoon of cinnamon
¼-teaspoon salt

Stir to blend then add ½-teaspoon soda. Stir briskly as the syrup will foam. This is when you must be careful as this syrup is extremely hot. Pour half of the mixture in the first pan containing popped corn and nuts. The remaining syrup will stay hot until ready to use for the second pan of corn. Use your spatula or wooden spoons to toss and stir until corn is evenly covered with syrup. Pour into prepared cookie sheet or broiler pan and place in a 200 degree oven. Repeat these directions for the second pan of popped corn.

Stir both pans of Cinnamon Carmel Corn every fifteen minutes for an hour. Turn the mixture of both pans onto a table covered with newspapers and foil. Let cool and break apart and store in jars or plastic zip lock bags. This recipe is one that is always included when I send gifts to my grandchildren. You will have plenty to share with family and friends.

HANNAH'S PEANUT BARS

I had to add this recipe as it was one my Mother Hannah made when I was a child which was about 70 years ago. I still remember what a great treat it was, the cinnamon flavor in the icing and the salted peanuts on the outside it was our treat instead of candy bars. During the 1930's we always made our candy at home like fudge, divinity and taffy, but these Peanut Bars were my favorite.

Bake either sponge or regular white cake in a long oblong pan that we called a sheet cake. My mother always made her cakes from scratch but you can use a box cake mix. Cut cooled baked cake in squares and frost with cinnamon icing.

CINNAMON ICING

Two cups sifted powder sugar
2-tablespoon butter-softened
½-teaspoon cinnamon

Add a few drops of milk or cream to make a smooth icing. Mix well. Grind salted peanuts and place in large flat dish. Ice cake squares on all four sides and roll in ground-salted peanuts. Set aside to firm up icing.

This was one of my favorite childhood memories of helping make these treats. We would have to grind the nuts with that old grinder you had to clamp on the table. It had all those different blades to be added to get the right texture of the ground salted peanuts. Many times we would sneak extra nuts on the sly, but I am sure my mother knew what was going on. Help your child to have pleasant memories and don't forget to use that cinnamon, it had a long and interesting life to get to your kitchen. I have continued to use cinnamon ever since and still love this wonderful spice.

CINNAMON CRAFT PROJECTS

LACE SACHETS HATS

I discovered these lace ornaments after my oldest sister sent me one from the crocheted doily my mother had made. I thought this was such a good idea that I had to make some myself. I did not crochet my own lace doily but purchased some from the craft store. The direction for making these lace sachets are, to soak the doily in liquid starch as used for starching clothes. Using plastic saran wrap on folded newspapers, center your doily over a small round object such as a Styrofoam ball. Drape your doily over the ball and arrange the edges to make a pleasing design

Let your doily dry completely it may take several days. Remove carefully from saran wrap including the ball. Fill hollow space with potpourri and glue a circle of felt or cardboard on the back to hold in your potpourri. Decorate the front of your doily sachet hat with ribbon, cinnamon beads, flowers, and hang your creations in a favorite place.

CINNAMON ORNAMENTS

I have experimented with cinnamon ornaments, after I saw the recipe below printed in our newspaper from Tones Spice Company. I received permission to use this recipe when I was in the process of writing this book, The Cinnamon Stick, a few years ago. I thoroughly enjoyed working with this recipe and still have these items hanging on my walls. It is amazing how long they keep that wonderful scent.

1-cup of ground cinnamon
1-teaspoon ground allspice
1-teaspoon ground cloves
1-teaspoon ground nutmeg
1-cup applesauce

Measure all spices in a 2-quart bowl and stir to blend. Add ½ cup applesauce and blend. Add remaining applesauce and blend to resemble play dough. If mixture is too dry, add ½-tablespoon of applesauce. If cinnamon mixture is too sticky, sprinkle working surface with ground cinnamon. Roll dough out to ¼-inch thickness using cookie cutters or paper patterns to cut our shapes. Using pencil make a hole in top or ornament to tie yarn or ribbon on your ornament when dry.

Place on folded newspapers to air dry, turning often until firm and completely dry. This may take a week. Attach ribbon or yarn and your ornament is ready for hanging. I have cut out large heart shapes for some wall hangings. I used cloth such as burlap or lace to imprint in the cinnamon clay for an added effect.

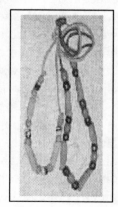

I have made beads and pendants from the cinnamon clay to make necklaces. Shape dough in different sizes of beads. Use a small dowel to put in the hole for stringing. Place beads on newspapers to dry for several days. String them onto leather or nylon cord in any desired arrangements and knot the ends of the cord for a finished necklace.

This Cinnamon recipe was printed in our Des Moines Register newspaper. I received permission form Nancy Pelley from the Tone Spice Company of Ankeny, Iowa to publish it. She asked to give them credit whenever I published this recipe. Be creative your children will have fun working on this for a Christmas gift project.

I wrote about my love of cinnamon in a review on epinions.com under the topic of "The Best Arts and Crafts Ideas" (this topic is now cancelled). Earlier in 2002 I received e-mail from Rochelle Beach who has a web site where she sells miniature cinnamon objects. Her web site is called (cinnaminnies.com.) She was interested in the history of cinnamon and suggested a book. After our many discussions I revised and expanded the original book into The Cinnamon Stick-Tales of the Spice Trade.

The photograph above is one of Rochelle's dolls, named Hannah. I purchased her as a remembrance of my mother who's name was Hannah. You will notice the little Hannah doll made of cinnamon by Rochelle can be found in some of the Cinnamon pictures included in this book. Experiment yourself with this recipe or send for "cinnaminnies" bulk supplies and test your creative instincts.

You get out of life just what you put into it…so add a little cinnamon.　　　Letta ☺

BIBLIOGRAPHY

Archer, Jules-Arabs, Little Brown – 1976
Archer, Jules-Legacy of the Desert, Little Brown – 1976
Bible-Revised Standard Version – World Pub. Co.
Ceram. C. W.-The Secrets of the Hittites. Alfred Knopf -1956
Cochran, Hamilton-Freebooters of the Red Sea Bobbs-Merrill 1965
Cottrill, Leonard-Land of the Two Rivers World Pub. Co. 1962
Day, Groves-Pirates of the Pacific – Meredith Press 1968
Davidson, Margaret-The Pirate Book – Random House 1965
DeCombray, Richard-Caravansary – Doubleday 1979
Doughty, Chas.-Travels in Arabia Deserta – Heritage Press 1953
Ewing, Joseph-The Ancient Way – Scribner 1965
Falls, C. B.-The First 3000 Years – Viking Press 1960
Frank, Irene-To the Ends of the Earth – Facts on File 1984
Habenstein, Robert-The History of Americana Funeral-Bulfin 1962
Hadas, Moses-Imperial Rome – Time-Life 1965
Hamlyn, Paul-Encyclopedia of Ancient & Medieval History-1964
Hargreaves, Pat-The Indian Ocean – Silver Burdett 1981
Hartman, Gertrude-Medieval Days and Ways – Macmillian 1937
Heritear, Jacqueline-Potpourri and other Fragrant Delights 1973
Hitti, Philip-Arab Civilization – St. Martin Press 1968
Ilian, M.-Giants at the Crossroads – International Pub. 1948
Irwin, Constance-Fair Gods and Stone Faces-St. Martin Press 1963
Jessups, Ronald-The Wonderful World of Archaeology-Doubleday
Laeng, Alexander-The Heritage History of Seafaring America 1974
Langdon, William-Everyday Things in American Life-Scribner
Lopez, Robert-The Commercial Revolution of the Middle Ages
Meade, Margaret-People and Places-World Pub. Co. 1959
Mellaart, James-Early Civilization of the Middle East 1965
Miller, Russell-The Seafarers-The East Indiamen-Time/Life 1980
Pfeiffer, John-The Search for Early Man-American Heritage 1963
Purseglove, J. W.-Spices Vol. I & II Longman Pub. 1981
Rosengarten, Frederic Jr.-The Book of Spices-Berkley Pub. 1969
Schulberg, Lucile-Historic India – Time/Life 1968

Seignobos, Charles-The World of Babylon 1975
Shaw, Stanford-History of the Ottoman Empire-Cambridge 1976
Sherrard, Philip-Byzantium-The Great Ages of Man-Time/Life
Simon. Dyanne-Commerce-The Barter Book-Dutton 1979
Skinner, Chas-Myths & Legends of Flowers, Trees, Fruits & Plants
Strong, Donald-The Early Etruscans – Putman 1968
Tannahill, Ray-Food in History – Stein & Day 1973
Thompson, Brenda-Pirates – Lerner 1977
Walsh, Richard-The Adventure & Discoveries of Marco Polo-1953
West, Anthony-The Crusades – Random House 1954
Winer, Bart-Life in the Ancient World-Random House 1961

NATIONAL GEOGRAPHIC ARTICLES

Ambercrombie, Thomas – Arabian Frankincense Trail 10/85
Ambercrombie, Thomas – Jordon: Kingdom in the Middle 2/84
Duplaix, Nicole – Fleas the Lethal Leaper 5/88
Judge, Joseph – Our Search for the Columbus Landfall 11/86
Judge, Joseph – This Year in Jerusalem 4/83
Miller, Peter – India-Unpredictable Kerala 5/88
Severin, Tim – Retracing the First Crusade 9/89
Severy, Merle – Byzantine Empire 12/83
Vesilind, Priit – Monsoons 12/81

ENCYCLOPEDIAS

Colliers Encyclopedia, P. F. Colliers & Sons 1947-1988
Encyclopedia Americana, Grolier Inc. 1980
Encyclopedia Britannica, Univ. of Chicago 1980
World Book, World Book Inc. 1988

BUSINESS AND ASSOCIATIONS

American Spice Trade Association – Englewood Cliff, NJ
McCormick & Company Inc. – Hunt Valley, Md
Tones Spice Company – Ankeny, Iowa

CPSIA information can be obtained at www.ICGtesting.com
Printed in the USA
LVOW081228101212

310899LV00001B/310/A